LEADING THE WAY THROUGH
JOSHUA

LEADING THE WAY THROUGH

JOSHUA

MICHAEL YOUSSEF

HARVEST HOUSE PUBLISHERS
EUGENE, OREGON

Cover design by Harvest House Publishers, Inc., Eugene, Oregon

Cover photo © iStockphoto / alexsl, BrianAJackson

Published in association with the literary agency of Wolgemuth & Associates, Inc.

Leading the Way Through Joshua

Copyright © 2013 by Michael Youssef
Published by Harvest House Publishers
Eugene, Oregon 97402
www.harvesthousepublishers.com

Library of Congress Cataloging-in-Publication Data

Youssef, Michael.
   Leading the way through Joshua / Michael Youssef.
      p. cm. — (Leading the way through the Bible Series)
   ISBN 978-0-7369-5168-5 (pbk.)
   ISBN 978-0-7369-5169-2 (eBook)
   1. Bible. O.T. Joshua—Commentaries. I. Title.
   BS1295.53.Y68 2013
   222'.207—dc23
                                        2012036688

*To all faithful preachers, teachers, and Christian leaders
who seek to faithfully expound the Word of God
from pulpits or in Sunday school classes or in home Bible study groups.*

Acknowledgments

I offer all my thanksgiving to the Father in heaven whose Holy Spirit has laid on my heart the writing of this series for the glory of Jesus. I am also immensely grateful to the Lord for sending me an able and gifted editor and compiler of my material in Jim Denney.

Special thanks to the entire team at Harvest House Publishers—and especially to Bob Hawkins Jr., LaRae Weikert, and Rod Morris, who shared my vision and made this dream a reality.

My expression of thanks would not be complete without mentioning the patience and perseverance of Robert and Andrew Wolgemuth of Wolgemuth and Associates, Inc. literary agency for managing the many details of such an undertaking.

My earnest prayer is that, as I leave this legacy to the next generation, God would raise up great men and women to faithfully serve their generation by accurately interpreting the Word of God.

Contents

Introduction

Trembling Heroes

Sergeant James Allen Ward was just twenty-two when he was called upon to do the impossible. During World War II, Sergeant Ward flew with the Seventy-Fifth New Zealand Squadron of the Royal Air Force. Based in England, he was a copilot aboard a Vickers Wellington twin-engine bomber.

On July 7, 1941, Sergeant Ward and his fellow crewmen flew a nighttime bombing mission over Münster, Germany. After the successful raid, the bomber was thirteen thousand feet over Holland when it was attacked by a German night fighter. The enemy plane approached within yards of the bomber's tail, cannons and machine guns blazing.

The bomber's rear gun turret was shredded by gunfire. The wounded tailgunner sprayed the enemy plane with machine gun fire. The Messerschmitt fell away and spiraled earthward, but its bullets had severed a fuel line, setting the starboard wing ablaze.

In the cockpit, the pilot told copilot Ward, "You've got to put that fire out!"

It was an order to do the impossible. How was Ward supposed to put out a fire on the starboard wing? If he didn't figure it out, the fire would spread and the crew would be forced to bail out over Nazi-occupied Holland. Ward didn't want to end up in a Nazi prison camp.

The pilot slowed the plane to just over a hundred miles an hour. Ward cut a hole in the side of the plane and tried to suppress the flames with a fire extinguisher—to no avail. When Sergeant Ward reported the failure, the pilot replied, "Prepare the crew to bail out."

"There's got to be something we can do," Ward said.

"You could go out on the wing and smother the fire," the pilot replied.

The idea was absurd. Ward wasn't a wing-walking stuntman! But then he thought about that Nazi prison camp and—

"I'll do it," he said.

He took a rope from the inflatable life raft and tied it around his waist, securing the other end to the airframe. Then he popped open a small Plexiglas dome on the top of the plane and squeezed through. A fellow crewman passed him a parachute, which he strapped on while clinging to the top of the plane. Then the crewmen handed him a folded canvas.

The skin of the bomber was amazingly thin, made of Irish linen stretched over the airframe and stiffened with lacquer. Sergeant Ward used his fists and boots to punch holes in the airplane skin to form handholds and footholds. As the crewmen paid out the rope, Ward climbed down to the wing.

He punched more holes in the wing and inched toward the burning engine. The winds buffeted him and the heat of the flames broiled his skin. He pushed the bolt of canvas in front of him and stuffed it into a flaming hole in the engine housing. Burning fuel sprayed around the edges of the canvas. Ward wondered if the canvas would ignite.

The flames went out!

Moments later, the canvas blew out of the hole and fell away into the darkness. Fuel continued to bleed from the severed fuel line, but the fire was out and the plane was saved. Ward made his way, handhold by handhold, across the wing, up the side of the plane, and back through the narrow hole in the top of the plane.

Nearly six hours after taking off, the plane approached the landing field. The pilot discovered that the flaps, used to maintain lift and slow the plane during landings, would not lower, so he had to bring the plane in too fast. As the plane touched the runway, the pilot found his brakes were gone as well.

The bomber rumbled off the end of the airstrip and plowed through a hedge. The impact destroyed the airplane—but the crew emerged alive.

A month later, Prime Minister Winston Churchill awarded James Allen Ward the Victoria Cross, the nation's highest honor for courage. As Sergeant Ward stood in the prime minister's office, Churchill asked him questions about his heroic achievement—but the airman couldn't speak. His knees knocked, his hands shook, and no words came out.

Churchill was amused. This brave young airman could crawl onto a burning airplane wing but couldn't speak to the prime minister. "Young man," he said, "you must feel very humble and awkward in my presence."

Ward nodded and managed to stammer, "Yes, sir!"

"Then you can imagine how humble I feel in your presence."

Sergeant Ward was a hero—even to the British head of state—because he accepted an impossible assignment, and he got it done.

Courage for impossible challenges

You and I may never be called upon to crawl across the flaming wing of an airplane, but we are called to face the crises and challenges of our times for the sake of our Lord. We are called to dare and to risk—even if we fail in the attempt. As someone once said, "God does not require you to win, but he does require you to fight."

There are times in our lives when God challenges us to take on a task that seems every bit as impossible as the challenge Sergeant Ward faced. When the time comes to dare great things for God, we have a choice to make: Do we trust God to strengthen us, to put a steel rod of courage in our spines, and to see us through this challenge? Or do we shrink back in fear and unbelief, rejecting God's call upon our lives?

That's the choice Joshua confronted in the opening verses of the book that bears his name. We first find Joshua mentioned in Exodus and Numbers, where he is mentored by Moses and sent out as one of twelve spies to explore the land of Canaan in preparation for conquest. By the time we arrive in Joshua 1, he has succeeded Moses as the leader of the people of Israel. Joshua, the son of Nun, of the tribe of Ephraim, was handpicked by God himself to take on the mantle of leadership. As commander of the army of Israel, Joshua led his people in their conquest of Canaan, the Promised Land.

The events described in the book of Joshua appear to be mentioned in several nonbiblical historical documents, including the cuneiform texts of the Akkadian Empire (Mesopotamia) and the Amarna Letters, a collection of ancient clay tablets discovered at Amarna in Upper Egypt. These records include appeals by Canaanite kings for military assistance from Egypt because of an invasion by the Habiru or Apiru people. Many scholars believe *Habiru* is a corrupted form of the word *Hebrew*. The Habiru are described as a fierce nomadic tribe of people who invaded the land of Canaan somewhere between 1800 and 1100 BC. The conquest of Canaan under the leadership of Joshua is generally dated at about 1400 BC.

The book of Joshua recounts the miraculous conquest of the heavily fortified city of Jericho, followed by both failure and success at Ai, the dramatic (and supernaturally aided) battles at Gibeon and the Waters of Mermon, and more. By the end of the book, Joshua—who was born a slave in the land of Egypt—has completed the "impossible" mission God had set before him. In the closing verses of the book, Joshua dies at the age of 110 and is laid to rest.

It's a thrilling chronicle of events, and the story of Joshua has much to teach us about how to live victoriously in the twenty-first century. Again and again, God calls Joshua and the nation of Israel to take on seemingly impossible challenges. The faithful choices Joshua makes are instructive for our lives. The principles that guided him are the same principles that will guide us to victory in the Christian life. Here is counsel and comfort for those times when we look to God and ask, "Lord, are you sure you're asking the right person? Are you sure you want me to do this? Do you realize you're asking me to do the impossible?"

Next to the Lord Jesus himself, there is no greater example of the spiritual traits of obedience, faith, and courage than this Old Testament hero, Joshua. As we study his inspiring example, we will learn to make the same faithful, courageous choices he made.

And we, too, will learn how to achieve the impossible.

1

Called to Step Up!

Joshua 1

L et me tell you a story about a man named Joshua.

No, not Joshua, the son of Nun, but Joshua Lawrence Chamberlain. He was a professor who taught at Bowdoin College in Maine in the 1800s. He was a scholar, a professor of modern languages, fluent in ten languages. Professor Chamberlain never studied military tactics, but when the Civil War came, he volunteered for the Union Army. His superiors recognized his brilliance and promoted him rapidly, so that he ultimately reached the rank of brigadier general.

He gained fame at the Battle of Gettysburg when he led the Twentieth Maine Volunteer Infantry Regiment at the defense of Little Round Top hill. The Union forces had suffered serious defeats on the first day of battle, and the Confederates pressed their advantage. Joshua Chamberlain knew that he and his regiment had to hold the hill at all costs. The Fifteenth Alabama Infantry Regiment charged again and again, inflicting many casualties on Chamberlain's men.

With ammunition dwindling, Chamberlain ordered a bayonet charge against the Confederates.

Though weak from a bout with malaria, Chamberlain led the charge. The Twentieth Maine came down the hill at the astonished Alabamans, who quickly surrendered. Chamberlain's men rounded up more than a hundred Confederate prisoners. Though Chamberlain suffered two gunshot wounds in the battle, he remained at the battlefront.

During his service in the Army of the Potomac, Joshua Chamberlain served in twenty battles and many skirmishes, had six horses shot from under him, was wounded in six separate battles, and was cited for bravery four times. Each time he was wounded, he returned to the battlefield at his earliest opportunity, often ignoring doctors' orders.

Joshua Chamberlain suffered his worst battlefield injury in the Siege of Petersburg, Virginia, where he was shot through the right hip and groin. Chamberlain resolved to set an example of utter fearlessness. He drew his sword, shoved the point into the ground, and leaned on it to remain upright as he shouted encouragement to his men. Eventually, loss of blood caused him to fall to the ground unconscious.

Soldiers carried him to a surgical tent, where the division surgeon determined his wound to be fatal. The next day, news of Joshua Chamberlain's death was reported by the newspapers across Maine. The citizens of Maine mourned the death of their scholar-hero. But a few days later, the newspapers were forced to print a retraction: Joshua Chamberlain *lived*—and he was soon back in command.

In early 1865, he was appointed commander of the First Brigade of the First Division, V Corps. His brigade won the battle on the Quaker Road, helping General Grant make his final advance to end the war. General Grant gave Joshua Chamberlain the honor of receiving one of the Confederate divisions during the surrender at Appomattox in April 1865.

After the war, Joshua Chamberlain returned to Maine and served as president of Bowdoin. I doubt that anyone who knew him as a professor of languages foresaw the legendary military career that lay ahead of him…or suspected that he would be wounded again and again, and keep running back to the battle…or that he would one day lean on his sword, bleeding profusely and encouraging his men until he lost consciousness.

Yet this Joshua, like the biblical Joshua, was a man who obeyed God's command: "Be strong and courageous!" Joshua Chamberlain died in 1914—a devout Christian, a paragon of courage, and a man worthy to bear the name of Joshua.

"Be strong and courageous!"

As the book of Joshua opens, Moses has died. So God goes to Joshua, the faithful right-hand man of Moses, and tells him, in effect, "Joshua, I want you to step up! I want you to lead my people into the land I have promised to them." The story begins:

> After the death of Moses the servant of the LORD, the LORD said to Joshua the son of Nun, Moses' assistant, "Moses my servant is dead. Now therefore arise, go over this Jordan, you and all this people, into the land that I am giving to them, to the people of Israel. Every place that the sole of your foot will tread upon I have given to you, just as I promised to Moses. From the wilderness and this Lebanon as far as the great river, the river Euphrates, all the land of the Hittites to the Great Sea toward the going down of the sun shall be your territory. No man shall be able to stand before you all the days of your life. Just as I was with Moses, so I will be with you. I will not leave you or forsake you" (1:1-5).

The Scriptures do not tell us in so many words that Joshua felt any reluctance to obey God's command. But I believe Joshua must have doubted that he was up to the task. God clearly finds it necessary to build up Joshua's courage and confidence.

When God calls any of his servants to a great challenge—whether that servant is named Joshua, the son of Nun, or Joshua Lawrence Chamberlain or [YOUR NAME HERE]—God always provides the encouragement we need to step up. As you can see in these verses, Joshua apparently needed a lot of encouragement (notice especially the phrases I have emphasized):

> "Be *strong and courageous*, for you shall cause this people to inherit the land that I swore to their fathers to give them. Only *be strong and very courageous*, being careful to do according to all the law that Moses my servant commanded you. Do not turn from it to the right hand or to the left, that you may have good success wherever you go. This Book of the Law shall not depart from your mouth, but you shall meditate on it day and night, so that you may be careful to do according to all that is written in it. For then you will make your way prosperous, and then you will have good success. Have I not commanded you? *Be strong and courageous*. Do not be frightened, and do not be dismayed, for the LORD your God is with you wherever you go" (1:6-9, emphasis added).

In these four verses, God tells Joshua, "Be strong and courageous," not one time, not two times, but *three times*. God sees Joshua perspiring and tugging at his collar. He sees that Joshua's knees are knocking together, so he gives Joshua a triple-dose of encouragement: "Be strong and courageous…Be strong and very courageous…Be strong and courageous." Then God adds a little extra encouragement for good measure: "Do not be frightened, and do not be dismayed." God encouraged Joshua in three significant ways:

First, *God encouraged Joshua through the promise.* God reminded Joshua of the promise he had made to Joshua's forefathers. "Be strong and courageous," the Lord said, "for you shall cause this people to inherit the land that I swore to their fathers to give them." God was referring to the promise he had made to Abraham six centuries earlier—and he had not forgotten his promise.

When you accept God's call to serve him and share his message with others, you can do so with courage and confidence because he has promised that he will never fail you. You don't have to worry that others will reject your witness. You don't have to wonder what others will think of you. You don't have to concern yourself with opposition or insults from your opponents. Why? *Because you trust in the promises of God.* You know that God always keeps his promises, and that is why you can confidently, obediently step up when he calls you.

Second, *God encouraged Joshua with the power of his Word,* commanding him to be careful "to do according to all the law that Moses my servant commanded you." God went on to say that his Word is powerful. If you obey it, you experience its power firsthand. If you dwell in it and apply it to your daily life, you will be prosperous and successful.

God is not promising that life will be easy for believers. As we shall see, Joshua faced setbacks, opposition, and crises—and so will we. But if we obey God's Word and hold our ground, we will stand firm even though others around us may crumble. True prosperity and success come from clinging obediently to the Word of God.

Third, *God encouraged Joshua by his presence*: "Do not be frightened, and do not be dismayed, for the LORD your God is with you wherever you go." If we read between the lines, we can surmise that, even after receiving these first two words of encouragement from the Lord, Joshua was still shaking at the knees. The Lord had reminded Joshua of his promise and his Word—but Joshua's confidence was still at low ebb.

So God gave Joshua a third word of encouragement. He said he would walk alongside Joshua throughout his battles and his crises. God knew what Joshua was thinking: *What good are promises and Scripture verses against a race of giants armed with swords and spears?* So God saved the most powerful word of encouragement for last, telling Joshua in effect, "You will not face your battles alone. I will stick closer to you than your own skin. I will be with you wherever you go."

On hearing these words from the Lord, Joshua was convinced. His courage was amply fortified. He said, "Yes, Lord, I'll step up. I'll do what you've called me to do."

What was the secret to victory in Joshua's life? The secret is simply that *there is no secret!* God has revealed *everything* to Joshua—and to us. When we live according to God's promises and his Word, and when we trust in his presence moment by moment, he will give us the victory—guaranteed!

Behind the eight ball with Joshua

I am the pastor of an Atlanta congregation called The Church of The Apostles, an evangelical congregation committed to declaring the whole counsel of God. We believe that nothing we do is as important as obeying the words of Jesus: "And this gospel of the kingdom will be proclaimed throughout the whole world as a testimony to all nations" (Matthew 24:14).

People sometimes ask, "Why do you call your church The Church of The Apostles? Is it because you believe in the teachings of the early apostles? Or is it because you believe that the people in your church have been sent out, as in the days of the apostles, as witnesses for Christ?"

I reply that *both* reasons are true. We believe in the foundational teachings of the Apostles (capital A)—and we also believe that we are *all* apostles (small a), "sent ones," called to be the Lord's witnesses in our community and around the world.

But there is yet another reason, a very different reason, that we are called The Church of The Apostles. When the church was founded in 1987, a man in authority in our former denomination told me that this would be the name of our church. We would have no say in the matter.

At that time, our church was under the Anglican denomination. Within that denomination are evangelical Christians who believe in preaching the gospel of the kingdom as a testimony to the world, in accordance with the command of the Lord—and there are also those who do not believe in preaching the gospel. The man in authority, the man who gave our church its name, did not believe in preaching the gospel. He disapproved of the evangelical stance of our congregation.

He looked me in the eye and said, "We don't need evangelicals and gospel-preaching churches in our denomination. Though we have agreed to allow you to start this church in Atlanta, there are two things I must tell you: First, don't quit your day job, because this church will fail in less than six months. Second, you are to name your congregation The Church of The Apostles. Since you are determined to start a congregation of people who want to spread an evangelical gospel, that is how you will be known."

"The Church of The Apostles" was intended by this man as a label of derision. We were being mocked for being a church filled with little evangelical apostles who practiced a quaint, old-fashioned faith and who preached a quaint, obsolete gospel.

When this man made it clear to me that he was giving our church a derisive name, I remembered that when the Lord's followers were first called "Christians" (meaning "little messiahs") at Antioch (see Acts 11:26), it too was a label of mockery and derision. And in the eighteenth century, when the teaching of John Wesley ignited a revival accompanied by evangelistic and missionary activity, the believers in that movement were mocked and ridiculed. Their critics called them a bunch of "Methodists" because they methodically practiced such customs as receiving communion, fasting, and abstaining from sin.

So I concluded that if our congregation was going to be labeled as an act of mockery because of our devotion to Christ and his gospel, then we were in excellent company with the great saints of the past. I trusted that God could use even our critics to accomplish his will. So I said to this man, "I am under authority. I will accept your direction. We will be called The Church of The Apostles."

That man passed away a number of years ago. Today, The Church of The Apostles, which was supposed to fail within six months, has been preaching the gospel of the kingdom since 1987. Over the years, The Church of The Apostles has had its ups and downs. But through it all, I always knew—and the congregation always knew—that this church was not Michael Youssef's idea. It was not the idea of any human authority or leader. It was the result of a decision by God. When God said, "Step up," we obeyed and we trusted in his promises.

In all that time, our mission hasn't changed. We still preach the gospel of the kingdom in the whole world as a testimony to all nations. Our vision hasn't changed; it has only been brought into sharper focus. We are still a church of apostles, a congregation of "sent ones," believers sent by the Lord Jesus into the offices, shops, schools, neighborhoods, mission fields, and battlefields of our world.

Like Joshua, we have been called by God to step up, to be strong and courageous, to accept the challenge, even though our knees are knocking. The Lord has promised us that we will accomplish our mission. If we trust in his Word and meditate on it day and night, we will be successful in carrying out the will of our Lord and Commander. God himself has promised us his presence and power—if we will step up.

God may be calling you to step up and accept a new challenge in your life. That's why you're reading *Leading the Way Through Joshua* right now. How did you happen to find this book (or how did it find you)? Did someone give it to you? Did you hear about it on the radio or TV? Did you just discover it by chance while browsing in the bookstore? However this book may have come into your possession, I don't believe it was an accident. God is challenging you to attempt something great in his name. He is calling you to step up and move out into a realm that he has promised you.

Perhaps there's a crisis, an opportunity, or a challenge in your life at this very moment. As you face this situation, you feel inadequate for the task. You lack confidence. You may even feel afraid. You are looking to heaven and saying, "Lord, you want me to step up and do *what*? But that's impossible! I'm not capable, I'm not qualified—and I'm scared!"

My friend, that's exactly where God wants you. You are standing in the very spot where Joshua himself once stood. You're asking God the same question Joshua once asked, and God's reply to you is still the same: "Be strong and courageous!"

Like Joshua, you are right at the threshold of a great work for God, and the first thing God wants you to do is *step up*!

Prophets and priests

In the Old Testament, God performed his work through prophets and priests. But in the New Testament, *all* believers in Jesus Christ are called to be prophets and priests.

What is a prophet? Most people think of a prophet as a person who foretells the future; but in the Bible, a prophet is not someone who *foretells*, but someone who *tells forth* the will of God. A prophet reminds the people of God's commandments, and he calls them to obedience, repentance, renewal, and transformation. In Numbers 11:29, Moses said that he wished "that all the LORD's people were prophets, that the LORD would put his Spirit on them!"

These words were fulfilled when Peter, quoting from the Old Testament prophet Joel, said,

> "'And in the last days it shall be, God declares,
>   that I will pour out my Spirit on all flesh,
>   and your sons and your daughters shall prophesy,
>   and your young men shall see visions,
>   and your old men shall dream dreams.'"
>
> (Acts 2:17)

Peter said this while speaking prophetically to a great crowd in Jerusalem. And when he called upon the people to repent and be baptized, three thousand people responded and became followers of Jesus Christ (see Acts 2:14-41).

Though the Holy Spirit has given some Christians a special gift of prophecy, God expects *all* of his people to speak out prophetically, to call others to repentance, and to share with them the good news of Jesus Christ. In a very real sense, all believers are called to be prophets.

And we are called to be priests. Peter wrote, "But you are a chosen race, a royal priesthood, a holy nation, a people for his own possession, that you may proclaim the excellencies of him who called you out of darkness into his marvelous light" (1 Peter 2:9). As a priest, you are called by God to minister to the people around you and to declare to them the glory and grace of God.

God has given you a unique mission to carry out as his prophet and priest. He has called you to undertake a task that only you can accomplish. No one else can do it for you. If you don't do it, it won't get done.

You cannot say to God, "I'm sorry, that task is not for me. You picked the wrong Christian. You need to find someone who is better suited to the challenge." If God has called you to do it, then he will equip you for the task and give you the confidence and courage to do it. When God calls us to do his work, he always gives us the encouragement we need, just as he encouraged Joshua three times. When he sets a challenge before you, all you have to supply is the obedience. God will supply the rest.

What is the impossible task God has called you to do? What does God want you to step up and accomplish as his chosen prophet and priest? Whatever that challenge may be, you now stand where Joshua stood. His leadership challenge and obedience challenge is now yours. His calling is now your calling. And the encouragement and strength God gave Joshua is now yours as well.

In Joshua 6, we will come to the story of Joshua and the city of Jericho. You're familiar with the story—so familiar that you may have forgotten what a powerful story it is. In the account, God not only gives Joshua an impossible assignment—conquer the most heavily fortified city in Canaan—but he also saddles Joshua with a hopeless strategy: The army of Israel is to march around the city once a day for seven days, then seven times in one day, then blow trumpets and shout. Does that sound like a winning military strategy to you? Or does it sound like absolute madness?

Imagine Joshua standing before the walls of Jericho, his mind clouded with doubts. *Lord,* he must have thought, *this is an impossibility! The walls of that fortress are impenetrable! Do you know what you are asking?* Yet, as we shall see, Joshua was obedient to God's call.

He accepted the impossible mission God had given him, and he accomplished it.

Perhaps the challenge God has set before you seems every bit as impossible as attacking a walled city with trumpets and shouts. The impossible mission God has given you might be to conquer your neighborhood, your workplace, or your campus with the good news of Jesus Christ.

Or your impossible mission might be to show love and grace toward one specific person—a relative, a neighbor, a colleague, a fellow student. That person might seem totally resistant to God's Word and uninterested in a relationship with Jesus Christ. Just as Joshua once faced the fortified city walls of Jericho, you may be facing a stone wall of rejection.

God may even be calling you to witness to your worst enemy. He may be challenging you to reach out to someone who has hurt you, crushed you, and mistreated you. Difficult people often seem completely self-sufficient on the outside while inwardly they are on the verge of collapse. That difficult person in your life is your Jericho. God has called you to reach out and, by the power of His Spirit, bring down those walls and conquer that Jericho.

This age of space exploration and the Internet may seem far removed from the age in which Joshua lived. Yet, at its core, life in Joshua's time was little different from life today. Joshua lived in a time of social crisis, political upheaval, moral indifference, and spiritual confusion. And yes, he even lived in an age of terrorism, as we do today. Our society is encircled by people who hate our faith, our values, and our way of life, and they are 100 percent committed to our defeat or destruction. They range from Islamic extremists to atheists and secularists.

Joshua and his people faced a similar threat wherever they went in the land of Canaan. Great walled fortresses like Jericho stood at various strategic locations throughout Canaan, the Land of Promise. Within those walls were enemies who sacrificed their own children to strange gods made of metal and fire. Those enemy societies posed a serious external threat to the people of Israel. That was the Jericho without.

But Israel also faced a Jericho within, a serious internal threat. Some within the camp of Israel disobeyed God's commands, and their disobedience threatened the lives and security of all the Israelites.

We, too, face an internal threat, a Jericho within. Within the church are many who love money or love this fallen world or love to be praised and accepted by the world—and they love these things more than they love God. These people call themselves Christians, but their "faith" is nothing but easy believism—what we might call "churchianity" rather than true biblical Christianity.

Churchianity has been around for a long time. As Protestant theologian H. Richard Niebuhr wrote in the 1930s, many Christians seem to believe that a "God without wrath brought men without sin into a kingdom without judgment through the ministrations of a Christ without a cross."[1] Indeed, Jesus himself said to the rich, self-satisfied church in Laodicea, "So, because you are lukewarm, and neither hot nor cold, I will spit you out of my mouth" (Revelation 3:16).

Increasingly, people around us are turning away from a belief in objective evidence and reason. They have abandoned rational thinking in favor of shallow emotions. They prefer to do what *feels* right than do what *is* right according to God's Word. Commentator George G. Hunter III describes our current culture this way:

> The Church, in the Western world, faces populations who are increasingly "secular"—people with no Christian memory, who don't know what we Christians

are talking about. These populations are increasingly "urban"—and out of touch with God's "natural revelation." These populations are increasingly "postmodern;" they have graduated from Enlightenment ideology and are more peer-driven, feeling-driven, and "right-brain" than their forebears. These populations are increasingly "neo-barbarian;" they lack "refinement" or "class," and their lives are often out of control. These populations are increasingly receptive—exploring worldview options from Astrology to Zen—and are often looking "in all the wrong places" to make sense of their lives and find their soul's true home.[2]

In the midst of such a culture, people are crying out for a few Christian believers who are committed and courageous, who are willing to step up and speak out as prophets and priests to our generation. Our world is crying out for a few believers who love God and his Word more than their own comfort.

Because you are reading these words, I believe God is calling you to step up. He has chosen you as one of his prophets and as one of his royal priests.

Content to live in the shadows

The book of Joshua opens with the words, "After the death of Moses." Moses is dead and God now calls on Joshua to step up. Here again, we see a parallel between the life of Joshua and our own lives.

In the past, we in the church have largely relied upon the clergy—ministers and evangelists and missionaries, people we think of as "professional Christians"—to do the work of spreading the good news of Jesus Christ. The church still needs preachers and evangelists, of course, but the day of the "professional Christian" is largely over. The era in which the people around us would listen to evangelists and preachers has passed. In a symbolic sense, Moses is dead. Now God calls us, as a generation of a twenty-first-century Joshuas, to step up and stand in the gap left by the death of our "Moses," the end of the era of evangelists and preachers.

Who is going to make a difference for God in today's world? You, the person reading this book. You, the stay-at-home mom. You, the businessman. You, the student. You, the healthcare worker or public safety worker or soldier or lawyer or engineer or journalist or educator or factory worker or retiree. Whatever your walk of life, wherever you find yourself, you are a twenty-first-century Joshua. You are the one God has commissioned for this task at this moment in history.

I know you have misgivings. I know you feel inadequate. You're thinking, *God wants me to step up and carry the gospel to the people around me? How can I do that? I'm not a leader, I'm not a preacher, and I'm certainly no Joshua. If I try to share the message of Christ with someone else, I'll just make a mess of things. I just want to be an everyday, ordinary Christian. I just want to mind my own business and go to church on Sundays and have my needs met.*

If that's how you feel, you're not alone. When Joshua heard what God wanted him to do, his heart probably jumped into his throat and stuck there. That's why God had to encourage him three times. I think Joshua was content to live in the shadow of Moses. When God said, "Step up," Joshua wanted to step back. But God's work would not be accomplished until Joshua filled the gap left by Moses.

The same is true in your life and mine: The work of the Lord in our generation will not be accomplished until you and I and all the other Joshuas of our day become true prophets and priests of our Lord. We begin by stepping up.

It's normal to feel inadequate. In fact, *God wants you to feel inadequate* in your own strength so that you will rely on him for all your needs. As Jesus said:

> "Therefore do not be anxious, saying, 'What shall we eat?' or 'What shall we drink?' or 'What shall we wear?' For the Gentiles seek after all these things, and your heavenly Father knows that you need them all. But seek first the kingdom of God and his righteousness, and all these things will be added to you" (Matthew 6:31-33).

When we accept God's call upon our lives and pursue his kingdom and his righteousness with a whole heart, then he will supply all of our needs according to his riches in Christ Jesus. So don't be anxious. God knows what we need. He won't let us down.

Perhaps you only became aware of God's call on your life as you have been reading these words. But God didn't call you to be his Joshua during the past half hour while you've been reading. Just as God spent forty years preparing Joshua for the conquest of the Promised Land, God has been preparing you for your great challenge. He called you by name before you were born. Throughout your life, he has been bringing people, experiences, and insights into your life that have shaped and equipped you for this very moment. He is encouraging you right now. He will continue to minister to you through his Word, his Spirit, and his people.

God's side of the equation

Every football fan in the 1970s knew the exploits of Miami Dolphins star running back Eugene "Mercury" Morris. He helped lead the Dolphins to three consecutive Super Bowls, including back-to-back victories in Super Bowls VII and VIII. He ran for exactly one thousand yards during the Dolphins history-making undefeated season in 1972.

Though Mercury Morris was nimble and sure-footed on the football field, he stumbled badly after retiring from the game. In 1982, he was convicted of cocaine trafficking and sentenced to twenty years in prison.

At the same time, halfway across the country, God was preparing a man named Art Fowler to have an impact on Mercury Morris's life. Art is an ordinary Christian with an extraordinary desire to reach people for Christ. He lives in Colorado, and he regularly shares the good news of Jesus Christ with those he meets. He'll often strike up a conversation about God with a stranger in a coffee shop or supermarket checkout line. Hundreds of people have come to know Christ through Art's informal ministry.

In 1982, Art opened the newspaper and read about Mercury Morris's conviction and sentence. Though Art had never met Morris, he knew the fallen football star needed to hear the good news of Jesus Christ. So he bought a plane ticket and flew to Miami. Once there, he talked his way into the Florida prison where Morris was held, and Morris agreed to meet with him.

Art sat down with Mercury in a visitation room at the prison and told him that, in spite of his imprisonment, God wanted to save him and use his life. "Mercury was open," Art recalls. "He was ready. And he prayed to receive Christ on the spot. Then he said, 'Art, I want you to go see my wife, Bobbie, and tell her what you just told me. I want my whole family to know about Jesus.'"

Art went to Mercury's house and explained to Bobbie that he had just visited her husband in prison. "She was there with her kids," Art recalls, "and we talked, and she accepted Jesus as the Lord of her life too."

In 1986, Mercury Morris's conviction was overturned by the Florida Supreme Court and he was granted a new trial. He reached a plea deal with the prosecutors that sentenced him to time served. Mercury Morris was a free man. Today he travels the country as a Christian motivational speaker.

In a TV interview, Mercury Morris recalled his life-changing meeting with Art Fowler. "I have a lot of trophies," he said. "They're all over the house. But the only trophies I have out on display are the ones that are the most significant to me. One of the things of significance I keep out is a plaque with a little football player on it that I got from Art Fowler back in 1987. It reads, 'I can do all things through Christ who strengthens me.'"

Mercury Morris and Art Fowler are teammates, playing on the same winning team with Jesus Christ, with Joshua, and with you and me. "Art Fowler is my teammate in the spiritual sense," Mercury says today. "Coach Don Shula and the Miami Dolphins, that's one thing. But Art Fowler and Jesus Christ, that's another."

What do you think would happen if every person reading these words became like Art Fowler? Imagine if there were thousands of Art Fowlers around this country, sharing the gospel with strangers in coffee shops and checkout lines and prisons, wherever and whenever God opened a door. How many lives would be changed as a result?

You may think, *I can't do that. I haven't even told my neighbors or coworkers I'm a Christian. I have never witnessed about Christ to a single soul. The very thought of talking to someone about Christ makes my knees wobble!* If that's how you feel, then you are in the same place Joshua was, looking at a fortified city and seeing a stone wall of impossibility.

What went through Joshua's mind when God told him to take that city in his name? The Israelites were a young nation of ex-slaves who had spent forty years wandering in the desert—a ragtag army of wandering tent-dwellers, ill-equipped for battle. They faced an ancient civilization with a long tradition of military might, defiant and secure behind walls of stone.

But there was one more factor on the Israelites' side of the equation: God himself. When the Lord issued his challenge, he told Joshua, "Do not be frightened, and do not be dismayed, for the Lord your God is with you wherever you go." When Joshua weighed all the factors on both sides of the equation, he knew everything he needed to know. And that's why, despite the impossibility of the task and his own inadequacy, Joshua accepted the mission. He stepped up because he had full confidence in his Lord.

Carried by the Lord

Nineteenth-century English preacher Henry Moorhouse had a daughter, Minnie, who was paralyzed from the waist down. Her affliction weighed heavily on his soul. He also felt oppressed by struggles and opposition in other areas of his life and ministry.

One day, Moorhouse came home with a package for his wife. As he entered the front door, he saw his daughter sitting in a chair. He bent down and kissed her, then said, "Where is Mother? I have a package for her."

"Mommy is upstairs," the little girl said. "Can I give her the package, Daddy?"

"Minnie, how can you carry a package? You can't even carry yourself upstairs."

"Daddy, that's easy! I'll carry the package while you carry me!"

Henry Moorhouse experienced a flash of spiritual insight. Even though he was carrying burdens in his life that seemed too heavy to bear, he was being carried by the Lord Jesus Christ. Together, they could bear the burden.

That's what God will do for you and me when we step up and

answer his call. No matter how impossible the challenge may seem, God will carry us. That was his promise to Joshua. It's still his promise to us today. The rest of Joshua 1 tells how Joshua and his people responded to God's call to step up and lay hold of the promise:

> And Joshua commanded the officers of the people, "Pass through the midst of the camp and command the people, 'Prepare your provisions, for within three days you are to pass over this Jordan to go in to take possession of the land that the LORD your God is giving you to possess.'"
>
> And to the Reubenites, the Gadites, and the half-tribe of Manasseh Joshua said, "Remember the word that Moses the servant of the LORD commanded you, saying, 'The LORD your God is providing you a place of rest and will give you this land.' Your wives, your little ones, and your livestock shall remain in the land that Moses gave you beyond the Jordan, but all the men of valor among you shall pass over armed before your brothers and shall help them, until the LORD gives rest to your brothers as he has to you, and they also take possession of the land that the LORD your God is giving them. Then you shall return to the land of your possession and shall possess it, the land that Moses the servant of the LORD gave you beyond the Jordan toward the sunrise."
>
> And they answered Joshua, "All that you have commanded us we will do, and wherever you send us we will go. Just as we obeyed Moses in all things, so we will obey you. Only may the LORD your God be with you, as he was with Moses! Whoever rebels against your commandment and disobeys your words, whatever you command him, shall be put to death. Only be strong and courageous" (1:10-18).

Joshua commanded the people to prepare to go into the Land of Promise and possess it. The people responded that they would obey Joshua just as they had obeyed Moses. God promised the land of Canaan to Israel. He promised to carry Israel across the Jordan River, past the walls of Jericho, and into a land that flowed with milk and honey.

But Israel had to step up. The Israelites had to trust in God, obey his instructions, and do his will. That is what the people committed themselves to do.

So it is with you and me. When God calls us to step up, we must obey and step up. We must answer the call and accept the challenge, knowing that God never issues a challenge without making provision for us to meet that challenge. God never gives a command without a promise. God has called you, and he will not abandon you or forsake you. We can step up in confidence and courage, knowing that even though our knees are knocking and our hands are trembling, he is with us.

2

Into Enemy Territory

Joshua 2

Eli Cohen was the most celebrated spy in the history of modern Israel. Born in Egypt in 1924, Cohen began working with Israeli military intelligence in 1960. Assuming the guise of a Syrian Arab named Kamel Amin Tsa'abet, Cohen established a false identity in Argentina, then moved to Damascus, Syria.

Cohen befriended many Syrian government officials, including Amin Hafiz, who eventually became prime minister. Cohen was so convincing that Hafiz actually considered appointing the Israeli spy as Syria's deputy defense minister.

Eli Cohen studied the Syrian fortifications on the Golan Heights, then made recommendations to the government that eucalyptus trees be planted around bunkers and artillery emplacements that targeted Israel. Cohen told the Syrians the trees would provide camouflage and shade. After the Syrian military took his suggestion and planted the trees, Cohen informed Israel's military intelligence. In the Six-Day War in 1967, the Israeli Air Force simply targeted the stands of newly planted eucalyptus trees—and they were able to easily destroy most of the Syrian military installations on the Golan Heights.

In January 1965, Soviet counterespionage agents tracked coded radio signals to Eli Cohen—and they arrested him. When he was discovered, Cohen was third in line to succeed Amin Hafiz as president of Syria. Cohen was hanged in Syria on May 18, 1965, but the information he provided before his death gave Israel the victory in the Six-Day War two years later. For his role in that victory, Eli Cohen is remembered as a hero in Israel to this day.

The story of Eli Cohen has many parallels to the spy story in Joshua 2. The biblical account describes an espionage mission that took place three thousand years ago when Joshua sent two Israelite spies deep into enemy territory—and their courageous exploits helped produce victory for the nation of Israel.

An Old Testament spy thriller

As this ancient tale of espionage opens, Joshua sends the two spies behind enemy lines, into the walled city of Jericho:

> And Joshua the son of Nun sent two men secretly from Shittim as spies, saying, "Go, view the land, especially Jericho." And they went and came into the house of a prostitute whose name was Rahab and lodged there (2:1).

God directed the two spies to the house of a dishonorable woman—a Canaanite prostitute named Rahab. The two spies saw her not as a prostitute but as a woman who desperately needed to be saved. So the spies made a bargain with her, telling her in effect, "Our lives for your lives! If you don't tell the Jericho authorities what we are doing, we will treat you kindly and faithfully when the Lord gives us the land."

The spies never lost sight of their mission. They had entered enemy territory to win a victory for God's cause—and to rescue Rahab and her family when they turned to the Lord for help.

I'm reminded of another Old Testament character, a man who went into enemy territory—but instead of going among the enemy people to serve God and save some of them from destruction, he became one of them. His name was Lot, and the enemy city he lived in was called Sodom. In Genesis 19, we see that, instead of living as a shining light for God in that dark city, Lot blended into the shadows of moral compromise. Instead of standing strong for God, he bargained away his integrity.

Unlike Lot, the two spies who entered Jericho accepted their mission as an opportunity to minister to the desperate need of Rahab and her family. They refused to compromise with sin and evil, because they had come to defeat it. The Scriptures go on to tell us:

> And it was told to the king of Jericho, "Behold, men of Israel have come here tonight to search out the land." Then the king of Jericho sent to Rahab, saying, "Bring out the men who have come to you, who entered your house, for they have come to search out all the land." But the woman had taken the two men and hidden them. And she said, "True, the men came to me, but I did not know where they were from. And when the gate was about to be closed at dark, the men went out. I do not know where the men went. Pursue them quickly, for you will overtake them." But she had brought them up to the roof and hid them with the stalks of flax that she had laid in order on the roof. So the men pursued after them on the way to the Jordan as far as the fords. And the gate was shut as soon as the pursuers had gone out.
>
> Before the men lay down, she came up to them on the roof and said to the men, "I know that the LORD has

given you the land, and that the fear of you has fallen upon us, and that all the inhabitants of the land melt away before you. For we have heard how the LORD dried up the water of the Red Sea before you when you came out of Egypt, and what you did to the two kings of the Amorites who were beyond the Jordan, to Sihon and Og, whom you devoted to destruction. And as soon as we heard it, our hearts melted, and there was no spirit left in any man because of you, for the LORD your God, he is God in the heavens above and on the earth beneath. Now then, please swear to me by the LORD that, as I have dealt kindly with you, you also will deal kindly with my father's house, and give me a sure sign that you will save alive my father and mother, my brothers and sisters, and all who belong to them, and deliver our lives from death." And the men said to her, "Our life for yours even to death! If you do not tell this business of ours, then when the LORD gives us the land we will deal kindly and faithfully with you."

Then she let them down by a rope through the window, for her house was built into the city wall, so that she lived in the wall. And she said to them, "Go into the hills, or the pursuers will encounter you, and hide there three days until the pursuers have returned. Then afterward you may go your way." The men said to her, "We will be guiltless with respect to this oath of yours that you have made us swear. Behold, when we come into the land, you shall tie this scarlet cord in the window through which you let us down, and you shall gather into your house your father and mother, your brothers, and all your father's household. Then if anyone goes out of the doors of your house into the street, his blood shall be on his own head, and we shall be guiltless. But if a hand is laid on anyone who is with you in the house, his blood shall be on our head. But if you tell this business of ours, then we shall be

> guiltless with respect to your oath that you have made us
> swear." And she said, "According to your words, so be it."
> Then she sent them away, and they departed. And she
> tied the scarlet cord in the window (2:2-21).

Word reached the king of Jericho that spies had entered the home of Rahab the prostitute, so he ordered Rahab to turn the spies over to him. But Rahab kept the Israelite spies hidden under stalks of flax on her rooftop. She sent word back to the king that the spies had escaped.

That night, Rahab went to the roof and helped the two Israelite spies escape from the city. Because her house was built into the city wall, she was able to let the two spies down by a rope from her window. Before the two spies melted into the darkness, they told Rahab that when the army of Israel returned to destroy the city, she should display a scarlet cord in the window. The Israelite soldiers would see the blood-red cord and spare her house and everyone inside.

The scarlet cord is a symbolic echo of the first Passover, when God, through Moses, commanded the Jews in Egypt to splash the scarlet blood of a sacrificial lamb on the doorposts of their homes. The angel of death would pass over the house without taking the life of the firstborn son of the household. The spies told Rahab to use a symbolic blood-red cord instead of the actual blood of a lamb, but the principle is the same: The Israelite soldiers, upon seeing that blood-red cord, would spare the inhabitants of that home—Rahab and her family.

Like the lamb's blood on the doorposts, the scarlet cord is a symbol of the blood of Jesus Christ. Those whose lives have been hidden in Christ, who are covered by the blood of the Lamb of God, who are protected by the symbol of the scarlet cord, will be saved from the destruction that is coming upon the world.

We are aliens

Even after Rahab helped the two Israelite spies to escape from Jericho, they still had seventy-two desperate hours ahead of them as they hid out among the hills while the soldiers of Jericho searched for them. The Scriptures tell us what the spies did next:

> They departed and went into the hills and remained there three days until the pursuers returned, and the pursuers searched all along the way and found nothing. Then the two men returned. They came down from the hills and passed over and came to Joshua the son of Nun, and they told him all that had happened to them. And they said to Joshua, "Truly the LORD has given all the land into our hands. And also, all the inhabitants of the land melt away because of us" (2:22-24).

The spies returned to Joshua with a confident report: The Lord had truly prepared the way for the Israelites to come in and possess the land. In fact, the pagan Canaanite people were *melting in fear* because of the Israelites!

How should we apply this ancient story to our lives today? Is this merely an Old Testament spy thriller? Or does the adventure of these two Israelite spies still speak to us across the centuries?

The story of Joshua 2 is the story of faithful, committed believers on a mission. And just like these two Old Testament spies, you and I are on a mission, sent by God behind enemy lines. And since you are on a *mission*, what else would you be but a *missionary*? Perhaps you never thought of yourself as a missionary before, but that's exactly what you are as a follower of Christ. And wherever you live and work and spend your time is your mission field.

So you must ask yourself, "Am I carrying out the mission God has given me? As I live and work in enemy territory, am I maintaining my focus on my mission, like those two Israelite spies in

Jericho? Or have I blended in with my environment like Lot? Am I achieving my mission or have I compromised my mission? Have I lost sight of the very reason God sent me into enemy territory in the first place?"

Imagine if the two Israelite spies had gone into Canaan and said to themselves, "These people are wealthy and powerful. They enjoy a lifestyle of luxury. Are we sure we ought to go to war against this city? I wouldn't mind having some of these luxuries for myself! Maybe we can make a deal with these people. Maybe we can blend in, stay awhile, and enjoy the good things this city has to offer."

But the spies refused to compromise their mission. They remembered that they had entered enemy territory in order to fulfill God's plan for his people and his kingdom. And that is a profound lesson for your life and mine.

We dare not forget that this world is not our true home. We are aliens, temporarily sent into enemy territory. Our citizenship is in heaven, not here, behind enemy lines. When we are in the neighborhood, the workplace, the marketplace, or on the campus, we are on a mission. We are fulfilling God's strategy.

So instead of compromising with the enemy culture that surrounds us, with all of its enticements and pleasures and luxuries that would divert us from our goal, we need to stay focused on our mission. We need to always remember the real reason God sent us into enemy territory. God doesn't send us merely as spies, but as a rescue team to save the lives of people like Rahab and her family.

In Matthew 1:5, we see that Rahab, the Canaanite prostitute, is included in the genealogy of Jesus of Nazareth. The two spies didn't know it, but by rescuing Rahab and her family, they were helping to fulfill Old Testament prophecy by preserving the lineage of the coming Messiah and proving that God is a sovereign God who shows no partiality. We may never know what God may choose to bring forth when we respond to him in obedience, but we do know that God has an eternal plan, and each of us has a vital part to play in that plan.

Who is your Rahab?

God has sent us into enemy territory to rescue the Rahabs in our midst. He has sent us to reach out to the despised and disreputable ones, to the least and the last and the lost. He has sent us to share the good news of Jesus Christ with prostitutes, prisoners, addicts, alcoholics, the poor and the aliens, and all others who are treated as an underclass in this world. He has also sent us to share the good news with the rich, the powerful, and the up-and-outers, because their lives are miserable and empty too.

We may not feel drawn to either the down-and-outers or the up-and-outers. We may not want to be around them. The two Jewish spies in Jericho probably didn't have a very high opinion of Rahab, the Gentile prostitute. But we have been sent to such people nonetheless. We have been sent to share God's love with them and to accept them right where they are (though we don't intend to leave them there).

We Christians often make the mistake of thinking that people need to clean up their lives before they can be saved. That's simply not true, as the Scriptures make clear. If people had to clean themselves up before coming to God, it would negate the grace of God. As the hymn "Just As I Am" tells us,

> Just as I am, and waiting not
> To rid my soul of one dark blot,
> To Thee whose blood can cleanse each spot,
> O Lamb of God, I come, I come.

Human beings do not have the power to rid their souls of even one blot of sin. It is God's job to cleanse human souls. Those who are stained and defiled by sin need only to accept and receive God's cleansing grace. They simply need to come "just as I am."

We do a great disservice to people by making them feel they must look like us, act like us, dress like us, and live like us before they can be saved. God help us, that is not the message of the gospel. The good news of Jesus Christ is that God has reached down to sinners right where they are. God saves—from the gutter-most to the utter-most. God redeems those whom the world says are beyond redemption. God never gives up on his own, not even those who have given up on themselves.

Jesus saved the prostitutes, the tax collectors, the adulterers, the ones the Pharisees thought were beyond the reach of God's love. The very fact that God chose to save a Gentile prostitute named Rahab, along with her household, serves as an encouragement to us all. God sovereignly selected Rahab to become one of the ancestors of the Jewish Messiah—the Christ who would take away the sin of the world.

No matter what you or I have done, God's grace is still available. No matter what your crime or sin, no matter how rebellious you may have been, no matter how deep your shame and regret, God can save you, redeem your life, and use you in a mighty way if you say yes to him.

And God makes the same offer to everyone around you—including people who have hurt you, people you simply can't stand. God desires to save and redeem your foul-mouthed boss, your immoral coworker, your addicted fellow student, your bitter atheist professor, your angry, obnoxious neighbor. No one is beyond the reach of God's grace—and he has strategically placed you in enemy territory so that you can be a witness and a blessing to the Rahabs who are all around you.

Of course, if we are to reach out and rescue the Rahabs in our midst, we must be distinct from them. If we share the gospel with our coworkers, then we must give them a reason to want our gospel. If our own lifestyle, our ethics, our speech, and our behavior are no different from theirs, then what do we have to offer them? What are we rescuing them from if our way of life is no better than theirs? If we are not distinct from the world around us, if we simply blend in, then we have compromised with the enemy—and all of our witnessing will fall on deaf ears.

So who is your Rahab? And how will you reach that person for Christ?

An astonishing statement of faith

As you think about this story, you may wonder, was it right for Rahab to lie in order to protect the spies? The answer is no. It is *never* right to do wrong, even with good intentions. The Bible reports Rahab's actions, but it does not approve them. At this point in her life, Rahab had heard about the God of Israel—but she had not yet experienced him.

This is important to remember in our own lives as we work and witness behind enemy lines. As you carry out your mission in your workplace, your neighborhood, or your school, you will be amazed at the people who respond to your witness. Some who seem indifferent or openly hostile to Christ will do an about-face. Some who seem opposed to you may actually be watching you, listening to you, observing how you respond under pressure, and testing the authenticity of your Christian witness.

Imagine the astonishment of the two spies when they heard this Gentile prostitute declare her faith in God when she came to them on the roof, told them she knew God had given Israel the land, and acknowledged that "he is God in the heavens above and on the earth beneath" (see vv. 8-11).

While it is important to be equipped for the task of witnessing, and while we should want to have as much understanding of the Scriptures as we can, we don't need a PhD in apologetics in order to share Christ with non-Christians. We simply need to trust that God goes before us, preparing the hearts of those who need him. That's why we pray that God will prepare their hearts, just as he prepared the heart of Rahab.

When Rahab shared her infant faith with the two Israelite spies, she gave them all the encouragement they needed to carry on with their mission. She told them that God had already terrified the Canaanites living in Jericho. Even in that ancient world, news traveled fast. The Canaanites had heard how the Lord dried up the water of the Red Sea so that Moses could lead the Israelites out of Egypt (see Exodus 14). The Canaanites had heard of the destruction of the two Amorite kings, Sihon and Og (see Numbers 21). Rahab clearly knew the residents of Jericho well, because she was aware of their moods, their fears, the stories they had heard about the Israelites. She told the spies that all they needed to do was to walk in and take the Promised Land away from the godless inhabitants.

Why were the Canaanites so terrified of this wandering band of former slaves? It couldn't have been the Israelites themselves that terrified the Canaanites. As Rahab's words show, the true object of the Canaanites' fear was Almighty God. While the other Canaanite people melted in fear before the God of Israel, one woman, Rahab the prostitute, made a choice to turn to God for refuge.

There are undoubtedly people within your sphere of influence who are at the same place Rahab was. God has prepared their hearts. He has drawn them to himself. And now he has placed you in a strategic position to reach them with the gospel. They have been living in fear and guilt, thinking, *I've heard that Jesus saves. I've heard that Jesus gives strength to the weak and liberates the addicted. I've heard he sets the prisoner free and heals the brokenhearted.*

They are waiting for you to tell them about Jesus. They want to hear you say, "Let me tell you my story. Let me tell you how Jesus set me free from shame, worry, fear, and hopelessness. Let me tell you how he forgave my sin and took away my guilt and gave me a new robe of righteousness that can never be taken away."

And when you tell your story to the Rahabs in your life, they will say to you, "Why didn't you tell me this before?" And you may have to admit, "I kept my mouth shut out of timidity and fear. I'm sorry."

Don't keep your mouth shut one day longer. Rescue the Rahab in your life. Point the way to mercy and forgiveness. The same overflowing grace that changed the heart of a Canaanite prostitute is available for all who receive it.

Know your enemy

Thirty centuries have come and gone since those two Israelite spies hid under sheaves of flax on a Jericho rooftop. During that time, the business of spying has grown much more sophisticated. Spies today employ a bewildering array of abbreviations to describe their intelligence gathering activities. There's COMINT (COMmunications INTelligence), which involves eavesdropping on phone calls. There's ELINT (ELectronic INTelligence), or intercepting electronic signals. IMINT (IMagery INTelligence) is spying by taking photos from airplanes or space satellites.

But ask any intelligence expert the most effective form of spying, and he will probably say HUMINT—HUMan INTelligence, the risky business of putting spies behind enemy lines. Intercepted messages and satellite photos can yield important information. But if you really want to know what's going on in enemy territory, you must have human spies on the ground, penetrating the government, observing military activities, and extracting information. Whether wars are fought with swords and spears or drones and smart bombs, the key to victory involves placing human beings on the ground behind enemy lines.

This principle is equally true when it comes to spreading the good news of Jesus Christ. While I am grateful for such technologies as radio, television, and the Internet, and I utilize them all, God wants to use his faithful soldiers on the ground to do the hard work of face-to–face-evangelism. Technology is no substitute for human interaction. God wants people who are willing to go into enemy territory and to reach people where they live. God wants people who are willing to plant their feet in Satan's territory and claim it for Jesus Christ. Our goal is to rescue lost human souls and free them from enemy oppression, which requires that we build relationships based on genuine caring, not on mass media.

Those who are not citizens of the kingdom of heaven are captives of Satan's domain. God calls us to go into enemy territory, to share the good news of Jesus Christ, and to rescue people from the control of Satan. C.S. Lewis put it this way in *Mere Christianity*: "Enemy-occupied territory, that is what the world is. Christianity is the story of how the rightful King has landed, you might say landed in disguise, and is calling us all to take part in a great campaign of sabotage."[3]

Our enemy, the object of our campaign of sabotage, is Satan. Don't think for a moment that God is calling you to attack any human being. Your unbelieving coworkers, your agnostic fellow students, and your antagonistic neighbors are not your enemies. They may treat you as an enemy. They may be hostile to the good news of Jesus Christ. They may even cheat you, bully you, lie about you, and make you miserable—but they are not your enemy.

The reason people behave in such hurtful ways is that *they are living under the enemy's power*. They are slaves to the enemy's dictates. That's why they exhibit the characteristics of the enemy.

But we must never forget who our true enemy is. As the apostle Paul told us, "For we do not wrestle against flesh and blood, but against the rulers, against the authorities, against the cosmic powers over this present darkness, against the spiritual forces of evil in the heavenly places" (Ephesians 6:12). Our enemy is Satan. He is the one we fight.

God has strategically positioned you in your family, your career, your neighborhood, and your community because he has a plan for your life. He has placed you in your mission field. Every human encounter in your life is a God-given opportunity for you to invade Satan's territory and win another battle for Christ. Every person you meet is someone who could become your brother or sister in Christ. Even your worst enemy could one day become your dearest friend in the Lord.

So when people attack you, don't retaliate. Love them with the love of Jesus Christ. See them with the eyes of Christ. Pray for them and ask God to use you to help set them free.

Then see how God answers your prayer.

From enemy to brother

In another book in this series, *Leading the Way Through Daniel*, I tell the story of an American flyer in World War II, Jake DeShazer, who took part in the raid on Tokyo in April 1942. But there's another side to the story, and I want to tell it to you now.

Though Jake DeShazer was raised in a Christian home, he had never received Jesus as his Lord and Savior. After the Tokyo raid, his bomber was running out of fuel, so Jake and his fellow crewmen bailed out over enemy-occupied China. Jake would later learn that, at the instant he was falling through the skies over China, his mother in far-off America was praying for him, not even aware that he was on a dangerous mission.

Jake came down in a Chinese cemetery and was captured by Japanese soldiers. He spent the rest of the war in a series of prison camps, where he was often beaten and kept in solitary confinement. Two years into his imprisonment, Jake's captors allowed him to have a Bible for three weeks. He read from Genesis to Revelation, and by the end of those three weeks, he had received Jesus as his Lord and Savior.

There is another story that intersects with the story of Jake DeShazer. It's the story of Japanese fighter pilot Mitsuo Fuchida. As a boy growing up in Japan, Fuchida had dreamed of becoming a samurai, a warrior who would bring glory to the Land of the Rising Sun. He graduated from military academy at twenty-one, and his superiors selected him to lead the surprise aerial attack on Pearl Harbor, December 7, 1941.

On that Sunday morning, Mitsuo Fuchida climbed into his plane and took off from the deck of a Japanese aircraft carrier. He led a force of nearly two hundred planes. At 7:49 a.m., he radioed the battle cry to his fellow pilots: "Tora! Tora! Tora!" In an attack that lasted less than two hours, Mitsuo and his fellow pilots destroyed two mighty American battleships, two destroyers, a minelayer, and 188 airplanes; they left ten other ships seriously damaged. The Japanese attack killed 2333 Americans and wounded 1139.

Leaving the scene of battle, Mitsuo and his fellow pilots celebrated a stunning victory over the Americans. Japanese losses were light—only twenty-nine airplanes lost and fewer than sixty airmen killed or wounded.

The attack brought the United States into the war, which lasted more than three and a half years. During that time, Mitsuo Fuchida fought many battles over the Pacific and narrowly escaped death many times.

In June 1942, he was on the aircraft carrier *Akagi*, undergoing emergency surgery for appendicitis. His doctor told him to stay in the ship's infirmary to rest, but when he heard the sound of battle, he ran up on the flight deck. The Battle of Midway had begun. American planes attacked his ship, and the bombs penetrated to the lower decks before exploding—to devastating effect. Everyone in the infirmary was killed in the attack. Mitsuo Fuchida survived the battle because he disobeyed his doctor's orders.

In the summer of 1945, Fuchida was in a city on the island of Honshu when he received orders to fly to Tokyo. He flew his fighter-bomber out of the city on August 5. Hours later, an American bomber dropped an atomic bomb on that city—the city of Hiroshima. Once again, Fuchida's life was spared, but the atomic bomb spelled defeat for Japan. Mitsuo Fuchida, who had dreamed of being a noble samurai warrior, was left embittered and disillusioned.

But for the American airman, Jake DeShazer, the end of the war meant freedom. He returned to the States, got married, and attended seminary. After graduation, he and his wife Florence moved to Japan as missionaries. He also wrote a leaflet, printed in Japanese, that told the story of his imprisonment, his conversion to Christ, and God's love for the Japanese people.

A few years after the end of the war, Mitsuo Fuchida was in a train station in Japan when someone handed him a leaflet—"I Was a Prisoner of Japan" by Jake DeShazer. Fuchida boarded the train and read the leaflet as the train pulled out of the station. As he read DeShazer's story, he wanted to know more about Jesus. A few days later, he bought a Bible and began reading. He was struck by the words of Jesus in Luke 23:34—"Father, forgive them, for they do not know what they are doing." One day in 1950, Mitsuo Fuchida received Jesus Christ as his Lord and Savior.

Fuchida immediately began sharing his newfound faith with other people. The first time he spoke at an evangelistic rally, five hundred people committed their lives to Christ. He became a preacher and people called him "the Billy Graham of Japan."

One day, Fuchida went to the home of the man who had written the leaflet that changed his life. When Jake DeShazer answered the door, the former pilot said, "My name is Mitsuo Fuchida." DeShazer invited him in and embraced him. The two former enemies were now brothers in Christ.[4]

God has called all of us as Christians to go into enemy territory. Our mission is not to search and destroy, but to seek and to save. God calls us to reach out to those, like Rahab, who are lost in sin and enslaved by Satan—and to bring them safely into God's kingdom of love.

3

The River of Impossibility

Joshua 3–4

Born in Russia in 1874, Chaim Weizmann was a Jewish biochemist who invented a process for producing the solvent acetone through bacterial fermentation. Educated in Germany and Switzerland, he pursued his scientific research in England.

While in England, Weizmann became a central figure in the Zionist movement. The Jewish people had been without a nation of their own ever since the Roman army under Titus sacked Jerusalem and destroyed the temple in AD 70. The goal of Weizmann and his fellow Zionists was to restore the Jews to their homeland.

During the 1920s, Weizmann was a friend to many Arab leaders, including King Faisal I of Iraq. He helped lay the groundwork for a Jewish society in Israel by working with Albert Einstein to establish Hebrew University in Jerusalem in 1921. After centuries of Diaspora (the dispersal of the Jewish people all around the world), the dream of Israel occupied Weizmann's life, even though the dream seemed unachievable.

In the early years of Weizmann's Zionist involvement in the late 1800s, he befriended British political leader Arthur Balfour. It was a frustrating relationship for Weizmann. Though Balfour supported the idea of a Jewish homeland, he wanted that homeland to be in Uganda, an African nation, not Palestine.

Weizmann argued that the Jewish people had historical ties to Palestine, the land of Abraham, Isaac, and Jacob. But Balfour insisted that one piece of land was as good as another, and the Jews should be happy to live in Africa.

Finally, an exasperated Weizmann said, "Imagine, Mr. Balfour, that I could move all Londoners to Paris. After all, Paris is a beautiful city—and as you say, one piece of land is as good as another. Would you and your fellow Londoners accept such an offer?"

"But Dr. Weizmann, we own London! It's already ours!"

"But Mr. Balfour," said Weizmann, "my people possessed the city of Jerusalem when London was a marsh."

The subject of Uganda never came up again.

In 1948, in accordance with UN Resolution 181, the independent Jewish State of Israel was established in Palestine. The "impossible dream" of a Jewish homeland became a reality—and Israel's first president was none other than Chaim Weizmann.

The river of impossibility

The "impossible dream" of a Jewish homeland was first given to Abraham at around 2000 BC when God promised Abraham, "And I will make of you a great nation, and I will bless you and make your name great, so that you will be a blessing. I will bless those who bless you, and him who dishonors you I will curse, and in you all the families of the earth shall be blessed" (Genesis 12:2-3).

This impossible dream was handed down to Isaac and Jacob,

then to Moses and Joshua. And now, as we come to Joshua 3, we find Joshua standing on the banks of the "river of impossibility," the River Jordan. Looking out across that river, Joshua must have been keenly aware of his own inadequacy and the inadequacy of his people. The Israelites were a band of formerly enslaved refugees. The task of leading them across the river to take possession of the land must have seemed utterly impossible.

And here is where our lives intersect with Joshua's. You and I have also faced many situations that seemed hopeless. Yet here we are! By God's grace, we made it. Looking back, we see that God himself enabled us to cross our rivers of impossibility. The experience was difficult and painful, yet it stretched our character and increased our faith as we saw God enable us to:

- survive that tragic loss
- recover from that life-threatening illness
- find joy again after that shattering betrayal
- obtain that seemingly unattainable university degree
- experience peace after a destructive family crisis
- feel whole again after being falsely accused

I'm sure you can testify that God has brought you through challenges and struggles that you would never have thought you could survive. The experience of facing impossibilities tends to change us in one of two ways: It either makes us stronger, or it destroys us.

Some people break under the strain of life's impossible challenges. Some enter the river of impossibility and are overwhelmed by the flood, swept away by the current. Others, like Joshua, face their rivers of impossibility knowing that even though they are inadequate, God is more than adequate. They know he will lead them through the deep waters and safely to the other side. Those who trust in God will stand at the riverbank and where others see only impossibility, they will say, "What an opportunity for God to accomplish something great in my life!"

God can use a river of impossibility to do great things in your life—but Satan also uses rivers of impossibility. He will use them to discourage us, to silence our witness, to keep us from sharing Christ with others. He will continually try to get us to focus on our impossibilities instead of the infinite power of God.

When you stand at the riverbank, as Joshua did, Satan will stand at your side, saying, "Look at that flood. Look how far it is to the other side. You can't cross that river! You'd be crazy to try." When you hear the voice of discouragement and defeat within, chances are it's the voice of Satan trying to turn you away from God's will for your life.

As Paul told Timothy, "For God gave us a spirit not of fear but of power and love and self-control" (2 Timothy 1:7). A spirit of defeatism does not come from the Lord. He desires our boldness and faith. He wants the people around us to see that one weak, inadequate human being can achieve the impossible through faith in the God of Infinite Possibilities.

In Joshua 3, we see three crucial steps that Joshua takes—three steps we must all take in order to cross the rivers of impossibility in our lives. Those three steps are:

Step 1: Commissioning (verses 1-4)

Step 2: Consecration (verses 5-13)

Step 3: Completion (verses 14-17)

Let's look at each of these three important steps.

Step 1: Commissioning

We previously saw that Joshua sent two spies into enemy territory, and the spies returned with a good report. As soon as Joshua heard the report, he commissioned his people to cross over the river of impossibility, the River Jordan. Why was the river impossible to cross? It was impossible—and impassable—because of the time of year.

Later, in Joshua 4:19, we will see that these events took place on "the tenth day of the first month," the Hebrew month of Nisan, which corresponds to March–April on our calendar. Why is this timing significant?

Had the crossing of the Jordan taken place at another time of year, cynics could have said, "People could easily swim across at that time of year." But in the month of Nisan, the snows are melting on Mount Hermon and the waters of the Jordan are treacherously deep. The current is so fast that anyone foolish enough to step into the river would be swept away. As the chapter opens, we read:

> Then Joshua rose early in the morning and they set out from Shittim. And they came to the Jordan, he and all the people of Israel, and lodged there before they passed over. At the end of three days the officers went through the camp and commanded the people, "As soon as you see the ark of the covenant of the LORD your God being carried by the Levitical priests, then you shall set out from your place and follow it. Yet there shall be a distance between you and it, about 2,000 cubits in length. Do not come near it, in order that you may know the way you shall go, for you have not passed this way before" (3:1-4).

Joshua, through his officers, told the people that they were to follow the ark of the covenant and the Levite priests—and they were to walk straight toward the deep and rushing river. What do you suppose the people said? I can imagine their response: "You want us to walk into that river? Couldn't we wait until summer, when the waters are not so deep? This is madness!"

But Joshua gave the people their marching orders, which came straight from God. He told them when they were to go, what they were to do, whom they were to follow, and at what distance they should follow. As the people faced their river of impossibility, Joshua reminded them that God had commissioned them to cross the river and enter the Land of Promise.

So it is with you and me. When we face our rivers of impossibility, we are tempted to forget that we have been commissioned by God himself. We are tempted to say, "On top of everything else that's going on in my life, I don't need any more challenges. This really isn't a good time for me to witness for Christ. Someday, when I'm not feeling stressed out, I'll serve God, but this just isn't a good time."

God is our Lord and we are his servants. He does not adjust his plans for our convenience. When he says "Go!" our job is to go. When God commissions us, it's the right time. It's the right purpose. He has placed the right person in our path. He has arranged the circumstances. He has commissioned us. Our job is to obey.

The Israelites were afraid and God understood their fear and doubt. That's why he gave the Israelites the powerful symbol of the ark of the covenant going before them. What was the ark? It was a sacred box that was built by God's command in Exodus 25:10-22. It contained:

- the stone tablets on which God had written the Ten Commandments—a reminder of God's law
- a jar of manna, the miraculous food God sent to feed the Hebrew people in the wilderness—a reminder of his provision
- the staff Moses had raised at the parting of the Red Sea—a reminder of God's protection

Most important of all, the ark of the covenant represented the presence of God among his people. By sending the ark out before the people, God symbolically said to them, "I am going before you. I shall prepare the way and be your guide. As you cross this river of impossibility, you have nothing to fear because I am with you."

God specified the distance between the ark and the people: "Yet there shall be a distance between you and it, about 2000 cubits in length" (3:4). A cubit was about 18 inches, so 2000 cubits would equal 3000 feet or 1000 yards. God was letting the people know that he was not like the king on a chessboard who waits in the back while sending the pawns out to fight and die. God leads the way, preparing and protecting. God's message, symbolized by the ark, was, "Don't be afraid. I am going ahead of you to make a way for you. Be strong. Be courageous. Follow me."

Step 2: Consecrating

After the commissioning came the consecrating. We see the act of consecration in the next few verses:

> Then Joshua said to the people, "Consecrate yourselves, for tomorrow the LORD will do wonders among you." And Joshua said to the priests, "Take up the ark of the covenant and pass on before the people." So they took up the ark of the covenant and went before the people.
>
> The LORD said to Joshua, "Today I will begin to exalt you in the sight of all Israel, that they may know that, as I was with Moses, so I will be with you. And as for you, command the priests who bear the ark of the covenant, 'When you come to the brink of the waters of the Jordan, you shall stand still in the Jordan.'" And Joshua said to the people of Israel, "Come here and listen to the words of the LORD your God." And Joshua said, "Here is how you

shall know that the living God is among you and that he will without fail drive out from before you the Canaanites, the Hittites, the Hivites, the Perizzites, the Girgashites, the Amorites, and the Jebusites. Behold, the ark of the covenant of the Lord of all the earth is passing over before you into the Jordan. Now therefore take twelve men from the tribes of Israel, from each tribe a man. And when the soles of the feet of the priests bearing the ark of the LORD, the Lord of all the earth, shall rest in the waters of the Jordan, the waters of the Jordan shall be cut off from flowing, and the waters coming down from above shall stand in one heap"(3:5-13).

When the time came to cross the river of impossibility, Joshua did not say to the people, "Well, folks, we're about to cross over into the land of our enemies. Sharpen your swords, polish your shields, and gear up for battle!" Nor did he say, "Let's all do some calisthenics! You need to limber up those muscles. You're going for a swim today." No, Joshua simply said, "Consecrate yourselves."

You may ask, "Why didn't Joshua prepare them for battle?" Answer: He did. He prepared them for *spiritual* battle. He prepared them for *supernatural* battle. He prepared them to fight a battle in the realm of the humanly impossible. You don't prepare for a spiritual battle by sharpening your sword or stretching your muscles. To be victorious over the river of impossibility, you don't need powerful weapons or physical strength. You need to be consecrated to God.

Consecration is the act of totally dedicating oneself to the service and worship of God. It's the act of setting oneself apart solely for God's own use. Consecration requires a complete surrender of the will. When you are consecrated, you cannot offer God any half-hearted commitment. Consecration is an all-or-nothing proposition.

God allows rivers of impossibility in our lives not merely to demonstrate his power in our trials, but also to bring us into a consecrated relationship with him. He wants us to be 100 percent devoted to him, holding nothing back. He wants us to examine our lives, purge those sins we have tolerated and rationalized in ourselves, and cleanse ourselves of idolatry and self-centeredness.

If you feel you have been going through the motions of being a Christian, if you have not been an effective witness for Christ in your workplace, school, or neighborhood, and if you have never led anyone to Christ, then ask yourself: *Am I consecrated to God?* If you honestly answer no, then it's time to consecrate yourself, as the Israelites consecrated themselves before crossing over into the Land of Promise.

Once you are fully consecrated, watch out! God will use you in a mighty way. You'll become dangerous for God. You'll deal a powerful blow to Satan. You'll cross the river of impossibility and set foot in the Promised Land of God's will for your life.

Step 3: Completion

The Israelites have *commissioned* and *consecrated*. Now they are ready for Step 3: Completion. They needed to complete the task God has commissioned them to do:

> So when the people set out from their tents to pass over the Jordan with the priests bearing the ark of the covenant before the people, and as soon as those bearing the ark had come as far as the Jordan, and the feet of the priests bearing the ark were dipped in the brink of the water (now the Jordan overflows all its banks throughout the time of harvest), the waters coming down from above stood and rose up in a heap very far away, at Adam, the city that is beside Zarethan, and those flowing down toward the Sea of the Arabah, the Salt Sea, were completely cut off. And the people passed over opposite Jericho. Now the priests bearing the ark of the covenant of

the LORD stood firmly on dry ground in the midst of the Jordan, and all Israel was passing over on dry ground until all the nation finished passing over the Jordan (3:14-17).

Imagine the thoughts that went through the minds of the Israelites—and especially the priests—as they approached the river. The priests were to be the first Israelites to step into the rushing waters, carrying the ark of the covenant. This is one of the greatest tests of faith in the Old Testament. The priests had to ignore the evidence of their eyes and simply obey God's command, trusting in his promises.

What do most of us do with the promises of God today? We underline them in our Bibles, but do we act on those promises? Do we step out in faith upon those promises? Do we dare great things for God in reliance on his promises? No, but we do underline them. What kind of faith is that? True faith is not just something we talk about. Faith is expressed in action. If we are not willing to act on God's promises, then how can we say we truly believe his promises?

I'm not saying you should take wild risks and reckless gambles. Faith is not risking everything on a whim. Faith is acting boldly and courageously on the rock-solid foundation of God's reliable promises.

You may feel hesitant as you stand on the riverbank. You may tremble as you take that step of faith. That's all right. As long as you are willing to get your feet wet, God is pleased with your faith. Keep moving in the direction of God's calling. As long as you can look to your river of impossibility and say, "I am crossing this river in Jesus' name," God will be pleased with your faith.

Take counsel of your faith, not your fears

General George S. Patton Jr. commanded military campaigns in North Africa, Sicily, France, and Germany during World War II. Once, when General Patton was in Sicily, a fellow officer praised him for his bravery in battle. Patton is reported to have replied, "Sir, I am not a brave man." He said he got sweaty palms at the sound of gunfire, but, he added, "I learned early in my life never to take counsel of my fears."

In late 1944, General Patton commanded the US Third Army as it drove toward the Saar River region on the French–German border. During the predawn hours of November 8, Patton awoke to the ear-shattering sound of an American artillery barrage raining shells on German infantry positions. Patton couldn't help wondering about the fear the enemy must have felt as the long-dreaded Allied attack had finally come.

That morning, Patton recorded in his journal that he was grateful that "I had never taken counsel of my fears," and "I thank God for His goodness to me." Patton was not a flawless man, but he was a man who refused to listen to his fears. He persisted in doing his duty in spite of his sweating palms.

Where do you find your courage? A believer's courage comes from faith in God. We find courage when we trust in God's power, his character, his promises, and his Word. If we have consecrated ourselves to the omniscient, omnipotent, and omnipresent God, what have we to fear?

Courage is one of the greatest manifestations of faith. Courageous faith trusts that God cannot make a mistake. Courageous faith knows that God cannot be wrong and can never be defeated. As the Scriptures remind us:

> By faith the walls of Jericho fell down after they had been encircled for seven days. By faith Rahab the prostitute did not perish with those who were disobedient, because she had given a friendly welcome to the spies.
>
> And what more shall I say? For time would fail me to tell of Gideon, Barak, Samson, Jephthah, of David

and Samuel and the prophets—who through faith conquered kingdoms, enforced justice, obtained promises, stopped the mouths of lions, quenched the power of fire, escaped the edge of the sword, were made strong out of weakness, became mighty in war, put foreign armies to flight. Women received back their dead by resurrection. Some were tortured, refusing to accept release, so that they might rise again to a better life. Others suffered mocking and flogging, and even chains and imprisonment. They were stoned, they were sawn in two, they were killed with the sword. They went about in skins of sheep and goats, destitute, afflicted, mistreated—of whom the world was not worthy—wandering about in deserts and mountains, and in dens and caves of the earth (Hebrews 11:30-38).

Notice that all of these demonstrations of great faith were also demonstrations of great courage. If you want to become a man or woman of courage, then become a person of faith. Build a daily habit of risking great things for God. Don't be reckless or foolish, but ask God, "What impossible challenge do you want me to dare for you today?" When you take that risk and accomplish that challenge for God, you will see your faith grow—and your courage will increase as well. As Ralph Waldo Emerson once said, "Do the thing you fear, and the death of fear is certain."

It doesn't take courage to attempt tasks that are easy and familiar. But it takes great courage to attempt the impossible and move into unknown territory. If you do not feel fear, then you can't demonstrate either courage or faith. So if you are afraid to do what God calls you to do—but you do it anyway—be grateful for God's affirmation! Your Lord is pleased by your courage. He's pleased with your obedient faith.

I'm sure the priests of Israel were filled with trepidation as they approached their river of impossibility, but they did not take counsel of their fears. They took counsel of their faith.

Living memorials

The Scriptures tell us that the Jordan River was at flood stage as the priests carrying the ark reached its banks. The moment their feet touched the water's edge, the water stopped flowing from upstream. In a miracle reminiscent of the parting of the Red Sea (Exodus 14), the waters piled up some distance away, creating a passageway of dry land. So the priests and the people simply walked across the dry riverbed and into the Land of Promise.

Cynics like to point out that there have been times in recorded history when the River Jordan has dried up, exposing the riverbed. For example, history records an earthquake on December 8, 1267, which left the Jordan dry for ten hours. Of course, that was in December, before the spring thaws had swelled the waters in the river. And on July 11, 1927, there was an earthquake that is said to have caused the Jordan to dry up for twenty-one hours. But that was in the summertime, long after the spring floods.

There are no recorded instances of the Jordan River drying up during the flood time of March-April—except this account in Joshua. The river of impossibility became passable because of a supernatural intervention by the hand of God. The people of Israel crossed that river by faith in God.

The moment the Israelites set foot upon the Promised Land, they experienced a realization: They could not go back. Once you begin walking by faith, there is no going back to the old way of life. There is no going back to the spiritual wilderness; you must stay on the path that leads to the kingdom. There is no going back to fear, timidity, and mediocrity; you must go forth boldly and courageously.

Once you have crossed the river of impossibility, your eyes are open to the needs of the lost. You cannot go back to ignoring those people and pretending they have nothing to do with you. You realize that God has placed them in your path for a reason, and you must share the hope within you.

God is calling you to face your river of impossibility, whatever it may be. He is calling you to take that step of faith, to get your feet wet, and to keep moving forward in reliance upon his promises. Your river and mine may be very different rivers, but God is calling us both to accept the challenge and cross over.

The story of the river crossing continues in Joshua 4. God tells Joshua to set up a memorial to commemorate the miraculous crossing:

> When all the nation had finished passing over the Jordan, the LORD said to Joshua, "Take twelve men from the people, from each tribe a man, and command them, saying, 'Take twelve stones from here out of the midst of the Jordan, from the very place where the priests' feet stood firmly, and bring them over with you and lay them down in the place where you lodge tonight.'" Then Joshua called the twelve men from the people of Israel, whom he had appointed, a man from each tribe. And Joshua said to them, "Pass on before the ark of the LORD your God into the midst of the Jordan, and take up each of you a stone upon his shoulder, according to the number of the tribes of the people of Israel, that this may be a sign among you. When your children ask in time to come, 'What do those stones mean to you?' then you shall tell them that the waters of the Jordan were cut off before the ark of the covenant of the LORD. When it passed over the Jordan, the waters of the Jordan were cut off. So these stones shall be to the people of Israel a memorial forever."

And the people of Israel did just as Joshua commanded and took up twelve stones out of the midst of the Jordan, according to the number of the tribes of the people of Israel, just as the LORD told Joshua. And they carried them over with them to the place where they lodged and laid them down there. And Joshua set up twelve stones in the midst of the Jordan, in the place where the feet of the priests bearing the ark of the covenant had stood; and they are there to this day. For the priests bearing the ark stood in the midst of the Jordan until everything was finished that the LORD commanded Joshua to tell the people, according to all that Moses had commanded Joshua.

The people passed over in haste. And when all the people had finished passing over, the ark of the LORD and the priests passed over before the people. The sons of Reuben and the sons of Gad and the half-tribe of Manasseh passed over armed before the people of Israel, as Moses had told them. About 40,000 ready for war passed over before the Lord for battle, to the plains of Jericho. On that day the LORD exalted Joshua in the sight of all Israel, and they stood in awe of him just as they had stood in awe of Moses, all the days of his life.

And the LORD said to Joshua, "Command the priests bearing the ark of the testimony to come up out of the Jordan." So Joshua commanded the priests, "Come up out of the Jordan." And when the priests bearing the ark of the covenant of the Lord came up from the midst of the Jordan, and the soles of the priests' feet were lifted up on dry ground, the waters of the Jordan returned to their place and overflowed all its banks, as before.

The people came up out of the Jordan on the tenth day of the first month, and they encamped at Gilgal on the east border of Jericho. And those twelve stones, which they took out of the Jordan, Joshua set up at Gilgal. And he said to the people of Israel, "When your children ask their fathers in times to come, 'What do these stones mean?' then you shall let your children know, 'Israel passed over this Jordan on dry ground.' For the LORD your God dried up the waters of the Jordan for you until you passed over, as the LORD your God did to the Red Sea, which he dried up for us until we passed over, so that all the peoples of the earth may know that the hand of the Lord is mighty, that you may fear the LORD your God forever" (4:1-24).

God tells the Israelites to take twelve stones from the riverbed and carry them to the place where they will camp for the night. There, in the encampment, they are to build a monument of stones. When future generations ask what those twelve stones mean, the Israelites are to say that "the waters of the Jordan were cut off before the ark of the covenant of the LORD. When it passed over the Jordan, the waters of the Jordan were cut off. So these stones shall be to the people of Israel a memorial forever" (Joshua 4:7b).

Like those twelve stones, our lives are to serve as living memorials to the power of God. When people ask us what our lives mean, we are to tell them, "By the sheer power and grace of God, I have crossed the river of impossibility. My life is a memorial to his grace forever."

So consecrate yourself, face your river of impossibility, and complete the work God has commissioned you to do. Let him make your life a living memorial to his grace.[5]

4

Willing to Yield

Joshua 5

Late at night on August 31, 1986, the Soviet passenger ship *Admiral Nakhimov* plowed the Black Sea with 888 passengers and 346 crew members aboard. The ship's pilot noticed that the *Admiral Nakhimov* was on a collision course with another ship and reported the situation to Captain Vadim Markov. The captain ordered the pilot to radio a warning to the other ship.

The message was received by the *Pyotr Vasev*, a massive Soviet freighter loaded with grain. Captain Viktor Tkachenko of the *Pyotr Vasev* radioed a reply: "Do not worry. We are aware of your course and we will miss each other." He did not change course.

Believing that the problem was resolved, Captain Markov went to his cabin to sleep. He left his second mate in charge.

Before long, however, the pilot of the *Admiral Nakhimov* realized that the two ships were still on a collision course. He sent warnings to the other ship, but the freighter didn't respond. The pilot begged the second mate to change course, but the second mate replied that the captain had told him to maintain the ship's heading.

Aboard the *Pyotr Vasev*, the captain—who had not taken the situation seriously before—suddenly realized that collision was imminent. He ordered the ship's engines to full reverse. At the same time, the second mate of the *Admiral Nakhimov* also realized that collision was imminent. He ordered a hard turn to port. Both orders came too late.

At 11:12 p.m., most of the passengers aboard the *Admiral Nakhimov* were sleeping. A few were on the promenade deck, stargazing or dancing to music. At that moment, the prow of the freighter knifed into the starboard side of the passenger ship, tearing a huge gash in the hull. The cold waters of the Black Sea poured into the engine and boiler rooms, knocking out the ship's power. The *Admiral Nakhimov* went dark and listed heavily to starboard, taking on water.

The passenger ship went down just ten minutes after being struck—and never launched a single lifeboat. Though more than eight hundred people were pulled alive from the water, more than four hundred perished. A commission of inquiry later placed full blame for those deaths on Captain Markov and Captain Tkachenko. The cause: human pride—a stubborn and mutual refusal to yield the right of way.

People hate to be told to yield. We don't like anyone getting ahead of us in line at the supermarket. We are enraged if someone cuts us off on the freeway. The idea of submitting to someone else or serving someone else makes us feel insulted and demeaned. It's our nature to refuse to yield to anyone—even to God himself.

The Bible is a "yield" sign

What are you supposed to do when you see this sign?

The yield sign tells drivers that, when they enter an intersection, they must slow down and stop if necessary to give another driver the right-of-way. Drivers who fail to yield may be cited and fined. The law takes yield signs very seriously.

As drivers, unfortunately, we don't always obey the yield signs. We are creatures of habit, and some of our driving habits can get us into trouble. If there is a yield sign along our daily drive to work or school, we sometimes become lax about obeying it. After a while, we don't even see it anymore. Only when we have an accident or we are cited by a patrolman do we ask ourselves, "Why didn't I yield?"

The sign is there for a reason. When you obey it, you drive safely and share the road with your fellow motorists. Ignore it, and you risk your own safety and the safety of others. You may get away with failing to yield for a while, but sooner or later the failure to yield will get you into trouble.

The Bible is filled with "yield signs." From Genesis to Revelation, the message of the Bible is, "*Yield* to God!" If you want a meaningful life, yield to God. If you want to know peace, joy, and contentment, yield to God. If you want an effective ministry and a fruitful witness, yield to God. If you want your children to know God and live for him, yield to God. If you want to experience victory in life's struggles, yield to God.

Yield to his will for your life. Yield to his commands and his gentle urging. Yield to the instructions in his book. Yield the right to control your life to him. Yielding isn't easy, it isn't fashionable, it isn't fun. But we will never be able to truly serve God and receive his blessings in our lives until we are fully yielded to him.

Rolling away the reproach of Egypt

A farmer and his wife traveled along a dirt road in the days of the horse and buggy. As their horse pulled them along a dangerous stretch of road, the woman became anxious. The road hugged the side of a steep hill, and the wife looked over the edge and saw a long drop to a river far below. In a moment of panic, she snatched one of the reins from her husband's hand.

The husband gently offered his wife the other strap of the reins.

"Oh, no!" the woman protested. "I don't want both reins! I could never manage that animal by myself!"

"In that case," the husband said, "you must make a choice. Either take both reins—or let me take them. Two people can't drive one horse."

Trusting her husband's experience, she yielded the reins to him, and they safely reached their destination. That is where we find the Israelites in Joshua 5. They had to yield the reins of their nation to God.

As the chapter opens, word has spread across the land of Canaan that the Lord has miraculously enabled the Israelites to cross the river. The kings of the Amorites and Canaanites are terrified of these former slaves who have entered their territory.

> As soon as all the kings of the Amorites who were beyond the Jordan to the west, and all the kings of the Canaanites who were by the sea, heard that the LORD had dried up the waters of the Jordan for the people of Israel until they had crossed over, their hearts melted and

there was no longer any spirit in them because of the people of Israel.

At that time the LORD said to Joshua, "Make flint knives and circumcise the sons of Israel a second time." So Joshua made flint knives and circumcised the sons of Israel at Gibeath-haaraloth. And this is the reason why Joshua circumcised them: all the males of the people who came out of Egypt, all the men of war, had died in the wilderness on the way after they had come out of Egypt. Though all the people who came out had been circumcised, yet all the people who were born on the way in the wilderness after they had come out of Egypt had not been circumcised. For the people of Israel walked forty years in the wilderness, until all the nation, the men of war who came out of Egypt, perished, because they did not obey the voice of the LORD; the LORD swore to them that he would not let them see the land that the LORD had sworn to their fathers to give to us, a land flowing with milk and honey. So it was their children, whom he raised up in their place, that Joshua circumcised. For they were uncircumcised, because they had not been circumcised on the way.

When the circumcising of the whole nation was finished, they remained in their places in the camp until they were healed. And the LORD said to Joshua, "Today I have rolled away the reproach of Egypt from you." And so the name of that place is called Gilgal to this day (5:1-9).

The Israelites have been wandering in the desert for forty years and all of the circumcised military men who came out of Egypt have died. The young men born during the forty years' exodus from Egypt are all uncircumcised. So, at God's command, Joshua orders the men of Israel to be circumcised and to remain in the camp until they are healed. Then God tells Joshua, "Today I have rolled away the reproach of Egypt from you." After the rite of circumcision, the Israelites celebrate the Passover:

> While the people of Israel were encamped at Gilgal, they kept the Passover on the fourteenth day of the month in the evening on the plains of Jericho. And the day after the Passover, on that very day, they ate of the produce of the land, unleavened cakes and parched grain. And the manna ceased the day after they ate of the produce of the land. And there was no longer manna for the people of Israel, but they ate of the fruit of the land of Canaan that year (5:10-12).

The Israelites celebrate the Passover, including unleavened bread made from grain harvested in Canaan. As soon as they begin living off food from the Promised Land, the Lord stopped sending manna, the heavenly food he miraculously provided for them in the wilderness. The moment the Israelites begin consuming the food of the Promised Land, they receive a foretaste of God's coming victory.

Joshua yields to a stranger

The nation of Israel has come home. They have entered the Promised Land, but they still do not possess the land. As they approach Jericho, Joshua receives a visit from a stranger who brings an amazing message:

> When Joshua was by Jericho, he lifted up his eyes and looked, and behold, a man was standing before him with his drawn sword in his hand. And Joshua went to him and said to him, "Are you for us, or for our adversaries?" And he said, "No; but I am the commander of the army of the LORD. Now I have come." And Joshua fell on his face to the earth and worshiped and said to him, "What does my lord say to his servant?" And the commander of the

LORD's army said to Joshua, "Take off your sandals from your feet, for the place where you are standing is holy." And Joshua did so (5:13-15).

The people of Israel were camped on the plains near the city of Jericho, and Joshua went out of the camp and looked across the plain toward the city, his military objective. The Scriptures don't tell us what Joshua's thoughts were at that moment, but he probably thought about his people, who had never experienced war before. Most had never even seen a fortified city. They had spent forty years wandering in the desert. Now God commanded them to conquer a mighty Canaanite stronghold. Joshua may have wondered if their faith and courage were up to the challenge.

As Joshua pondered the coming battle, he saw a man standing before him with a gleaming sword in his hand. (A little later in this chapter I'll explain who this man was.) Alarmed, Joshua asked, "Are you for us—or for our enemies?"

The stranger replied, in effect, "I have come to you as the commander of the army of the Lord. I'm not here to take sides. I'm here to take over."

Then Joshua fell on his face in reverence before the man and asked, "What does my lord say to his servant?"

The stranger replied, "Take off your sandals from your feet, for the place where you are standing is holy." So Joshua yielded and removed his sandals.

God does not beg us to yield. He doesn't suggest that we yield. He doesn't offer us bribes or inducements to yield. He says "Yield," period. He demands our yieldedness, and we must obey.

Why does God demand that we yield? He does so for our good—and for his glory. Why, then, do we refuse to yield? It's because in our fallenness our will is bent toward rebellion, not obedience. Amazingly, we will stubbornly resist God's will even when we know we are bringing harm to ourselves. Because our natural tendency is to rebel, he must often go to the trouble of taking away all other options. Out of his love for us, he must often make us so miserable that we have only one option left—the option to yield.

A husband and wife in our church once felt God urging them to host a backyard Bible club in their home as an evangelistic outreach to neighborhood children. Even though they both felt God's urging, they resisted. From a purely human perspective, they had good reason to resist.

This couple had two children, a three-year-old and a two-month-old. Their children kept them very busy, and they didn't see how they could take on the commitment of a backyard Bible club. As time went on, they realized that resisting God's urging was making them unhappy and dissatisfied. They knew what they had to do, so they yielded to God's urging. With the help of two other couples from church, they hosted the Bible club and invited kids from around the neighborhood. They put flyers in mailboxes, and they wondered if anyone would show up.

The first club event came—and more than fifty kids showed up! All of those kids got to hear the good news of the love of Jesus. And as a result of that Bible club, nine moms from the neighborhood began attending a Bible study for young mothers. Why did this happen? It happened because one Christian couple overcame their resistance and made a decision to yield.

When you yield yourself to God, he will use you—guaranteed! He will prepare a ministry for you in your neighborhood, your workplace, or your campus. Yield to him fully, holding nothing back. Yield to him spiritually, giving him all your worship and devotion. Yield to him emotionally, making him Lord of your joys and sorrows, your laughter and anger, your courage and your fears. Yield to him mentally, feeding your mind on the thoughts of God rather than the depraved and destructive ideas of this corrupt world. Yield to him physically, so that your body will truly be his temple.

To be yielded is to be consecrated. As we saw in the previous chapter, consecration precedes conquest. Yielding precedes harvesting. When we are consecrated and yielded to God, he will bless us and make us victorious.

Circumcision and Passover: symbols of yieldedness

How did the Israelites under Joshua's leadership demonstrate their yieldedness to God? Perhaps the most striking symbol of their yieldedness was the act of circumcision (vv. 2-9). From a human perspective, this would seem to be the height of insanity. The men of Israel were about to go to war. So what did God tell them to do? He told them to perform a painful ritual that would leave the men physically incapacitated for days.

What was the point of this ritual? Why were religious rituals even necessary? Why should the people of Israel carry out such seemingly pointless and painful acts? There is one answer to all of these questions: The people of Israel needed to yield to God.

It would be easy to yield to God if he never asked us to do anything difficult, costly, risky, or perplexing. If we yield only when it's easy and pleasant to do God's will, then we're not really yielding at all. It is yielding only when we give up our way to go God's way. If God is God, then we must yield even when it's hard to yield, even when it costs us everything to yield, and even when God's will makes no sense to us.

What is God asking you to yield to him? There might be something in your life that has become your idol. It has become a hindrance in your devotion to God. It might be a habit, a pastime, a goal, a career, a possession—and you clearly sense that God is calling you to yield that idol to him.

The thing God wants you to yield has dug its claws into your soul—and that's why God wants you to give it up to him. We all have our idols. God's will for our lives is that we surrender those false gods to him. God will not ask anything of you that is more unreasonable than what he asked of Joshua and his fellow Israelites. On the eve of the greatest battle any of them had faced, God told them they needed to be circumcised. Joshua and his men yielded themselves totally to God in this area of their lives—and God gave them the victory. If you are fully yielded to God, he will give you the victory, just as he made Israel victorious over Jericho.

Divine logic is unfathomable to the human mind because our perspective is limited while God's perspective is limitless. What was God's logic in ordering the men of Israel to be circumcised? What was the divine reason for physically incapacitating the men of Israel on the eve of battle? It makes no sense to us, but to God it makes perfect sense—and here's why: *God didn't want his people to think they had won the battle in their own strength.* He wanted them to know that he had given them the victory.

When God strips from us the last vestige of our personal strength, it may feel like a personal defeat—but in reality, it is the beginning of God's supernatural victory in our lives. As long as we are relying on our own power and resources, we are not relying on him. He will not take away our free will, but he will allow us to flounder and fail in our own strength, if that is what we choose. But he will continue to call to us and urge us to yield so that we can experience the victory he has planned for us.

The Israelites who had crossed the Jordan into the Promised Land were born in the wilderness. Only a handful, such as Joshua and Caleb, remembered what it was like to live in slavery in Egypt. Only those few remembered what it was like to cross the dry riverbed of the Red Sea. Only those few recalled what it looked like and how it felt to see the mighty Egyptian army swallowed up by the crashing waters of the Red Sea.

The generation that crossed into the Promised Land had never been circumcised. These people had never received in their flesh the sign of the covenant God had made with Abraham. They had never participated in the Passover.

The first Passover, of course, was in Egypt when the lamb was slaughtered and the blood was sprinkled on the doorposts. At the first Passover, the angel of the Lord passed over Israel and spared the firstborn sons (see Exodus 12). The second Passover was observed at Mount Sinai (see Numbers 9). In Joshua 5, we see the third observance of the Passover—a reminder of God's mighty deliverance of his people from Egypt.

The first Passover in Egypt was God's act of delivering his people. The second Passover at Mount Sinai was a reminder of this deliverance. The third Passover on the plain of Jericho was a reminder of God's past deliverance *and* a symbolic foreshadowing of an even greater deliverance—the deliverance from sin—that would come through Jesus the Messiah.

In much the same way, the sacrament of Holy Communion, the celebration of the Lord's Table, is both a reminder and a foreshadowing. It reminds us of God's past deliverance and salvation through the death of Jesus the Messiah at Calvary. It also reminds us that God continues to save his people in the present. And it foreshadows the coming day when we gather around his table in heaven.

Christ in the Old Testament

What did it mean when Joshua encountered the commander of the heavenly army? This is one of the most profound and exciting passages in all of Scripture. Many theologians believe that Joshua experienced a theophany, an appearance of the preincarnate

Christ. The man who stood before Joshua was probably the Lord Jesus in human form, appearing centuries before his incarnation at Bethlehem.

This same preincarnate Christ also appeared to Abraham under the great trees at Mamre (see Genesis 18). He appeared to Jacob at Peniel (see Genesis 32). He appeared to Moses in the burning bush (see Exodus 3). He appeared with his chariots of fire to Elisha and fought the Assyrians on Elisha's behalf (see 2 Kings 6). He was the fourth man in the fiery furnace with Shadrach, Meshach, and Abednego (see Daniel 3). And here, in Joshua 5, the preincarnate Christ appears before Joshua with his sword drawn.

The stranger calls himself "the commander of the army of the LORD." This is important because Joshua needs to know that when the people of Israel go up against the fortress that is Jericho, they do not go alone. The army of the Lord goes with them. You and I also need to know that Jesus, the Son of God, the commander of the Lord's army, goes with us into all the battles of our lives. The hosts of heaven are always ready to be deployed on your behalf and mine. The moment you yield to the Lord's call upon your life, he will deploy his forces on your behalf.

So take the sandals off your feet. Yield to the Lord of hosts, for the place where he has sent you—your neighborhood, your workplace, your school—is holy ground. Yield your desires, your opinions, your comfort zone, your self-indulgence, your time and talent and treasure, your self-pity and bitterness. Yield it all to him, and allow him to deploy the armies of heaven to aid you and bring you victory.

The Scriptures tell us that when Satan rebelled and was cast out of heaven, one-third of the angelic hosts fell from heaven with him, swept away by Satan's mad rebellion (see Revelation 12:4). This means that two-thirds of the angelic hosts remained loyal to God, and they are ready to be deployed on behalf of yielded believers. For every demon who wars against your soul, two of God's angels are fighting on your behalf. As the writer to the Hebrews tells us, "Are they not all ministering spirits sent out to serve for the sake of those who are to inherit salvation?" (Hebrews 1:14).

So go to your Commander-in-Chief and say, "Lord, I yield all that I am and all that I have to you. Take my yielded life and use it as you see fit."

Evangelist William Moses Tidwell (1879–1970) told the story of a man who wanted to come to God but couldn't bring himself to yield everything. This man would come to Tidwell's evangelistic meetings and would walk forward when Tidwell gave the gospel invitation—but though the man would pray and pray, he would leave the front of the church feeling discouraged and troubled. "I'm not ready to yield all," he'd say.

One day, the man came forward as he had done many times before. He prayed and prayed—and finally threw his hands in the air and shouted, "All right, Lord! I yield! Colt and all, Lord! Colt and all!" When he shouted those strange words, his face beamed with joy. "Thank you, Lord!" he shouted. "At last, I know I'm saved!"

Someone asked him, "Why did you shout, 'Colt and all, Lord'?" The man explained that he was the owner of a stable of racehorses. He had sensed that God wanted him to give up his racehorses because they were associated with the vice of gambling. The man was willing to give up racing and had sold off most of his horses—but there was one fast colt he couldn't release.

"I just wanted to see that horse race one time," he explained. "So I told God I would give up the racing business, but first I wanted to see this colt run in one race. Though I prayed and prayed and tried to make a deal with God, I had no peace. I knew what God wanted from me. So I finally surrendered everything to him—colt and all. And at that moment, I knew I was saved."

God cannot be the Lord of anything in our lives until he is Lord of everything. When we yield to him, he will come to us—not to take sides but to take over. He will prepare the hearts of our hearers, and he will give us the words to speak. He will bless our work and make us productive for him. He will encourage us and meet our needs.

And he will give us the victory.

5

The Strange Logic of God's Program

Joshua 6

Even skeptics of the Bible admit that the destruction of the ancient fortress-city of Jericho was no myth. It is a fact of history, convincingly attested to by archaeological evidence. Today, Jericho is a little village of twenty-five thousand people located in the West Bank. That little village stands on the site of the ancient walled city on the plain near the Jordan River—a city that was once a citadel of idolatry and military might.

The name of the ancient city is believed to be derived from *yerach* ("moon") because Jericho was famed for its shrines to pagan moon gods and goddesses. The origins of the city are shrouded in mystery.

The first scientific excavations of ancient Jericho were conducted by two German archaeologists, Ernst Sellin and Carl Watzinger, in 1907. Their discovery of Jericho's ruined walls confirmed that the city had been destroyed in a way that was consistent with the

Old Testament account. In fact, the walls appeared to have been destroyed so completely that the only "natural" explanation is a powerful earthquake.

The site was excavated in the 1930s by British archaeologist John Garstang of the University of Liverpool. Professor Garstang found evidence of an intense fire that had consumed the city at the time the walls collapsed. Structures along the inside of the wall were burned to the ground and there was a thick layer of ash and charred debris over everything. The destruction of the city was scientifically dated at somewhere between 1600 and 1400 BC—around the time of the events recorded in Joshua.

Many other Canaanite cities have been excavated in that same region. All appear to have been destroyed at around the same time as Jericho. So when we read this account in Joshua, we are not reading a myth, as skeptics would have us believe. We are reading the true account of how the Israelites of old overcame fear, committed themselves to God's program, and toppled Satan's domain.

The divine program

As we look at the story of Joshua and the siege of Jericho, we again see clear parallels between his time and ours. Like the Canaanite world, our world is permeated by immorality and idolatry. Atheism, paganism, and false religion are on the march. Truly, we live in Jericho times.

Living in such morally and spiritually corrosive days, it would be easy to give in to fear. It's tempting to look upon the fortress of Satan's domain and say, "The enemy is too powerful. Satan's fortress walls are too strong. Why even try?"

That's the mindset Satan wants for us—a mindset of fear and defeat. Our enemy knows he doesn't stand a chance against us if we live by faith in Jesus, our Commander-in-Chief. With confidence in our Lord, we can topple fortresses of addiction, temptation, lust, hate, abuse, division, racism, and more. Trusting in Jesus, we can reclaim our neighborhoods, workplaces, marketplaces, and schools for him.

As Joshua 6 opens, we see the gates of Jericho shut and barred. The Canaanites within the walled city are terrified of the Israelites. Jericho is a city under siege:

> Now Jericho was shut up inside and outside because of the people of Israel. None went out, and none came in. And the LORD said to Joshua, "See, I have given Jericho into your hand, with its king and mighty men of valor. You shall march around the city, all the men of war going around the city once. Thus shall you do for six days. Seven priests shall bear seven trumpets of rams' horns before the ark. On the seventh day you shall march around the city seven times, and the priests shall blow the trumpets. And when they make a long blast with the ram's horn, when you hear the sound of the trumpet, then all the people shall shout with a great shout, and the wall of the city will fall down flat, and the people shall go up, everyone straight before him." So Joshua the son of Nun called the priests and said to them, "Take up the ark of the covenant and let seven priests bear seven trumpets of rams' horns before the ark of the LORD." And he said to the people, "Go forward. March around the city and let the armed men pass on before the ark of the LORD."
>
> And just as Joshua had commanded the people, the seven priests bearing the seven trumpets of rams' horns before the LORD went forward, blowing the trumpets, with the ark of the covenant of the LORD following them. The armed men were walking before the priests who were blowing the trumpets, and the rear guard was walking after the ark, while the trumpets blew continually. But

> Joshua commanded the people, "You shall not shout or make your voice heard, neither shall any word go out of your mouth, until the day I tell you to shout. Then you shall shout." So he caused the ark of the LORD to circle the city, going about it once. And they came into the camp and spent the night in the camp (6:1-11).

Joshua gave the orders, and the people did as the Lord commanded. As the people of Israel marched around the city walls, Joshua reminded them to remain silent until he gave the order to shout. The Canaanites within the city, who were already terrified of the Israelites, must have been beside themselves with fear at this eerie, silent spectacle. Day after day, these strange people from beyond the river marched in silence around Jericho. There were no war cries, nor even any whispers—just the strange and ominous sound of marching.

And what did the Israelites think as they marched around the city? Surely, they must have wondered what kind of battle plan the Lord had in mind. They must have doubted the sanity of Joshua himself. Yet, in spite of their doubts, they did as the Lord commanded through his servant Joshua.

Why did God have the Israelites perform this strange ritual? The whole exercise seems pointless. Is there some sort of magic in the act of marching around the city? Certainly not; God does not practice magic. Was God engaging in psychological warfare against the Canaanites? Of course not—the Canaanites were already terrorized, and this silent march was hardly needed to induce further panic.

God always has sound, logical reasons for his actions and commands, even if we are unable to grasp his logic at the time. I believe the purpose of this ritual was not to impress the Canaanites but to teach the Israelites. God made them walk around those walls to convince them that there was no hope of conquering Jericho by human might or strategy. He wanted the Israelites to know they had no hope but God alone.

You may have been going through a time of trial in your life that seems completely hopeless. Perhaps you feel you are marching around the walls of Jericho, again and again, accomplishing nothing and wondering if there is any point in going on. Perhaps God is trying to teach you the same lesson he taught the Israelites. Perhaps he wants you to understand that your only hope is in him. He may be waiting for you to admit that this "Jericho" in your life is too powerful for you.

But no enemy is too powerful for God. He is waiting for you to turn to him and say, "I trust you to topple those walls. I can do nothing in my own strength. My hope is in you. Please pour out your power and blessing on me. Go before me, Lord, and win this battle—and I will give you all the glory."

The Israelites who marched in silence around Jericho had come to the end of their own resources. They were forced to rely solely on the power of God. As you sift through the pages of the Old Testament, you'll never find a time when the Hebrew people demonstrated greater faith than right here in Joshua 6. The previous generation of Israelites died in the wilderness because of their lack of faith. They murmured and complained against God. That's why they never lived to see the Promised Land. But this new generation said no to fear and yes to faith.

As I write these words, my prayer is, "Lord, may our generation in the twenty-first century be like the Joshua generation. May we exhibit the faith and courage of Joshua's people, and may we enjoy the same thrilling victory over Satan's stronghold."

Joshua's people could well have asked, "Lord, why are you making us tramp around these walls? Your strategy makes no sense. The Canaanites are battle-hardened warriors with advanced weapons and armor! We're just a bunch of wandering ex-slaves. Exactly how do you propose that we conquer the city by marching around in silence for seven days? What do these silly rituals have to do with the price of beans in Babylon? You want us to follow your divine program—but your program makes no sense!"

There are challenges and tasks that God calls you to perform that probably seem every bit as irrational. You can't understand why God's program often seems to make no sense. Why has God placed you in a job you hate, with a boss who mistreats you, with coworkers who are cruel to you? Why has God placed you in a classroom with an atheist professor who daily ridicules your faith? Why has God placed you in a neighborhood with needy, dysfunctional families living on either side of you? Why has God allowed your business or ministry to fail? Didn't he promise you a victorious Christian life? Yet his program for your life seems to make no sense.

Your struggles may fill you with doubt about God's plan and program for your life. The Scriptures do not tell us what was going through Joshua's mind, but I suspect he must have had doubts about God's program for Israel. Yet Joshua didn't act according to his doubts. He acted according to his faith. He responded with obedience. He committed himself and his people to the divine program.

Unless faith is expressed in action and obedience, it's nothing but talk. If God said, "Do it," then Joshua did it. Joshua put his trust in God's wisdom, not human logic. He obeyed his Commander-in-Chief.

The fortress of fear

For thousands of years, one of the most vexing problems for military strategists has been, How do you conquer a fortress? The one feature that defines a fortress is its thick, impenetrable walls. All the great cities of ancient times were surrounded by walls of stone.

Stone walls not only defended cities from attack, but made a strong statement to potential enemies: Look upon these walls and despair! This fortress is invincible. Don't even *think* of attacking!

The great unconquerable Sumerian city of Uruk boasted walls that were four stories high. The walls of Babylon were flanked by towers and surrounded by moats; when Cyrus the Great conquered Babylon, his forces sneaked into the city through water culverts beneath the walls. The Hittites built their stone-walled cities on hills and mountains so that any would-be invader would have to scale the hillside as well as the walls.

To conquer an ancient fortress, an invader had to lay siege, surrounding the city, cutting off commerce, and keeping the inhabitants holed up for months or years. Laying siege to a walled fortress was a difficult and expensive operation requiring great patience and determination. That's the kind of fortress Joshua and the Israelites faced on the plains of Jericho: Unyielding. Invulnerable. Invincible. The walled city of Jericho was a fortress of fear that defied all invaders.

It's interesting to compare the Old Testament story of the siege of Jericho with the principles of spiritual warfare in the New Testament. You may be surprised to learn that the name Joshua (in Hebrew, *Yehoshua*) is the equivalent of our Lord's name, Jesus (an anglicized Greek form of *Yehoshua* meaning "Jehovah saves"). So Joshua and Jesus shared the same Hebrew name.

When Jesus spoke of establishing his church, he used imagery that suggested the kind of battle Joshua and the Israelites faced at the walled fortress of Jericho. In Matthew 16:18, Jesus described his church as a mighty army that would lay siege to the fortress of hell itself, and he declared that "the gates of hell shall not prevail" against his church. The forces of hell are holed up behind walls and gates, but God and his church surround the walls of Satan's kingdom, and the gates of hell cannot withstand our assault. The victory of God's church is already assured.

The problem is that we often fail to realize that we have already won the victory through Christ. We forget that our Lord has promised that the gates of hell will fall before us. We pull back in fear because we lack the faith to believe our Lord's promise of total victory. The great English Bible teacher Captain Reginald Wallis put it this way: "The triumphant Christian does not fight for victory; he celebrates a victory already won."

It's true. Christ has already won the victory. All we have to do is obey God and take possession of the land. What is your Jericho? What is the towering, menacing obstacle that blocks your path to victory? What keeps you from claiming your mission field, your street, your office, or your campus for Christ? What is the fortress of fear that keeps you from carrying out the divine program God has planned for your life?

Do feelings of inadequacy hold you hostage? Are you held back by some past hurt you're unwilling to forgive? Are you afraid of rejection? Are you afraid of what people will think of you if you speak up for Christ? Are you afraid of embarrassment or of making a mistake? Are you afraid that God will let you down?

If we are honest with ourselves, we have to confess that all of these fears are rooted in disobedience. The Scriptures tell us again and again that we are not to be anxious or timid about speaking up for Christ. We are not to worry about what others think, and we should never be ashamed of the gospel of Christ. We should be quick to forgive and quick to seek forgiveness. So if any of these issues are holding us back, it is truly our disobedience that hinders our witness.

I would never trivialize the power of fear. I have experienced raw, heart-pounding fear on several occasions, and I know it's one of the most demoralizing emotions in human experience. Our fears can become a prison more escape-proof than Alcatraz. It's no sin to experience fear when we face a genuine threat. But a pattern of habitual timidity robs us of our joy and our effectiveness for God. The Lord wants to move us beyond fearfulness to a place of absolute trust in him.

Fear and faith are like the opposite ends of a seesaw. When fear is up, faith is down. When faith is up, fear is down. The stronger our faith, the weaker our fears.

Courage is not the absence of fear; courage is fear that is controlled by faith. When our emotions are ruled by faith, fear cannot control us. Only a fool has no fear in a dangerous situation—but people of faith and courage do not let fear rule their lives. As John Wayne once said, "Courage is being scared to death but saddling up anyway."

When we demonstrate the courage that comes from faith, we often find ourselves in hot water. We find ourselves facing criticism, mockery, opposition, and even physical threat. The heroes of the Old and New Testaments often faced danger and persecution as a direct result of their outspoken faith.

God does not guarantee our safety. We may experience persecution, hardship, or death because we have taken a faithful stand for him, but we know that God has won the ultimate victory. He gave his people the victory over Jericho—and he used the most unlikely methods and people (including a pagan prostitute!) to achieve that victory. And he will give you the victory over the Jerichos in your life as well.

The courage that comes from faith keeps us going even though we are puzzled by our circumstances, or straining under an unbearable burden, or trudging through the valley of the shadow of death. It's not easy to follow God's program for our lives, but we can trust our Almighty God to equip us and strengthen us for battle. He will never make a mistake. Even in our suffering, we are victorious because our eternal dwelling place is in heaven. We are confident because Christ has won the greatest victory and that is the foundation of our courageous faith.

God may not call you to the mission field or the battlefield, but he always calls us to step out of our comfort zones. He always calls us to act in courageous faith, even if only to summon the courage to share Christ with a neighbor over coffee. So step out in courageous faith. Take an obedient risk for Christ and his kingdom. Tithe your income even when you have all sorts of needs. Like Joshua and the Israelites, we must say no to fear and yes to God's program. Satan's fortress of fear is no match for our God.

Backward, Christian soldiers

In previous eras of church history, Christians viewed themselves as God's soldiers, locked in spiritual combat. Followers of Christ saw themselves as warriors for Christ—and not in a vague metaphorical sense but literally so. Early believers viewed themselves as part of a mighty army under the command of Jesus. That's why Christians in times past sang bold, militaristic hymns like "A Mighty Fortress Is Our God," "Battle Hymn of the Republic," and "Onward, Christian Soldiers."

Today, the church shies away from such militant themes even though our enemy is Satan himself. George Verwer, founder of the missionary group Operation Mobilization, satirized the mindset of much of modern Christendom when he penned a parody of "Onward, Christian Soldiers." In his version, the song begins, "Backward Christian soldiers, fleeing from the fight / With the cross of Jesus nearly out of sight."[6]

Those words may provoke an embarrassed smile and a wince of

recognition because there's a good deal of truth in that parody. The church today does seem timid, afraid, and in retreat before the enemy. Our courage has faltered because we have allowed our faith to falter.

What is God's answer? "Get with my program." And what is God's program? "Trust in me. Study the Word I have given you. Spend time with me in prayer, worship, and intimate fellowship. Get to know me. Learn to recognize my voice when I speak within your spirit. Become sensitive to my guidance for your life."

When we get with God's program and develop true intimacy with him, we will truly know what the prophet Isaiah meant when he said, "And your ears shall hear a word behind you, saying, 'This is the way, walk in it,' when you turn to the right or when you turn to the left" (Isaiah 30:21).

For some of us, getting with God's program means we overcome our shyness and our fear of what others will think of us. We stop letting golden opportunities for witnessing slip away from us. We demonstrate boldness and courage as we seize the opportunities God brings our way.

But for others, getting with God's program means speaking less and loving more. It means we stop barging blindly into every situation and preaching a fire-and-brimstone sermon to everyone we meet. Sometimes God calls us to listen and to love and to keep our mouths shut for a while. Some people need to experience the love of God, as expressed through sensitive caring, before they will respond to the Word of God. Every human soul is unique, and we should not apply a one-size-fits-all approach.

I'm from the Middle East. I know a little bit about the Middle Eastern temperament, so I think I can identify with Joshua and the Israelite people. I believe one of the hardest challenges the Israelites faced in getting with God's program was that God commanded them to be silent. God said, in effect, "No talking—for a week!"

Telling people from the Middle East not to talk is like telling a fish to stop swimming. The Israelites had to march around the walls of Jericho without talking, day after day after day. By the third or fourth day, the silence must have been killing them!

Remember, the Israelites were not one big homogeneous group. Israel was made up of twelve tribes that frequently quarreled with each other. To get with God's program, they had to stop bickering and start marching in unison. They had to stop complaining and arguing and demanding their own way. The fact that Joshua got all twelve tribes to march in lockstep was a miracle in itself.

And that's a lesson to us today: Are we twenty-first-century Christians any less quarrelsome and divided than the ancient Israelites? How well do Christians from various theological backgrounds get along? How well do Christians of this or that local church get along?

Do you remember what Jesus prayed for just hours before the cross? He asked the Father that his followers "may all be one, just as you, Father, are in me, and I in you, that they also may be in us, so that the world may believe that you have sent me" (John 17:21). Jesus prayed that we would be unified and undivided because our unity would serve as a witness to the world. Jesus prayed that Christians would be united in prayer, in worship, in fellowship, in mission and purpose, in tithing and giving, in serving and witnessing, and in love for one another. That is God's program for the church. That is how we are to reach out and reclaim our neighborhoods, workplaces, and schools for Christ. If we would truly practice Christian love and unity, we could transform our cities, our nation, and our world.

Faith in action

General George Patton had an unusual method of selecting officers for promotion. In *General Patton's Principles for Life and Leadership*, Porter B. Williamson tells how Patton would take a group of officers behind a warehouse and say, "I want you to dig a trench on that spot. Dig it eight feet long, three feet wide, and six inches deep." Then he would leave the officers alone to carry out their work.

What the men didn't know was that Patton would slip into the warehouse and eavesdrop on their conversation while they worked. Some would complain, "This is grunt work. It's demeaning to make an officer dig trenches!" Others would say, "The old man must be nuts! We've got machines that could dig this trench in two minutes!" And others would say, "Why six inches? What is he going to do with such a shallow trench?"

But there was almost always one man who would say, "Who cares what the old so-and-so wants to do with this trench? The sooner we get the job done, the sooner we get out of here!" That was the man Patton selected for promotion. A leader who could take orders was a leader who could give orders.[7]

God is looking for men, women, and young people who are willing to put their faith to work by acting in obedience to his will. When we obey God, he manifests his purpose in our lives. When we do the possible, God takes care of the impossible. When we carry out his strategy, no matter how illogical it may seem to us, he gives us the victory.

Down through the years, generals and military historians have studied the book of Joshua, looking for the tactical and strategic secrets behind Joshua's victory over Jericho. They have asked, "Where was Joshua schooled in the military arts? Certainly, there must be some hidden lessons of war to be gleaned from the siege of Jericho."

But there is no hidden lesson. The Word of God says what it means and means what it says. Joshua's victory over Jericho was not won by superior strategy or military might. It was won by obedience to the plan of God. It was won because Joshua and the people of Israel got with God's program.

A curse and a blessing

The closing verses of Joshua 6 tell us of the obedience of Joshua and the Israelites—and the destruction of Jericho:

Then Joshua rose early in the morning, and the priests took up the ark of the LORD. And the seven priests bearing the seven trumpets of rams' horns before the ark of the LORD walked on, and they blew the trumpets continually. And the armed men were walking before them, and the rear guard was walking after the ark of the LORD, while the trumpets blew continually. And the second day they marched around the city once, and returned into the camp. So they did for six days.

On the seventh day they rose early, at the dawn of day, and marched around the city in the same manner seven times. It was only on that day that they marched around the city seven times. And at the seventh time, when the priests had blown the trumpets, Joshua said to the people, "Shout, for the LORD has given you the city. And the city and all that is within it shall be devoted to the LORD for destruction. Only Rahab the prostitute and all who are with her in her house shall live, because she hid the messengers whom we sent. But you, keep yourselves from the things devoted to destruction, lest when you have devoted them you take any of the devoted things and make the camp of Israel a thing for destruction and bring trouble upon it. But all silver and gold, and every vessel of bronze and iron, are holy to the LORD; they shall go into the treasury of the LORD." So the people shouted, and the trumpets were blown. As soon as the people heard the sound of the trumpet, the people shouted a great shout, and the wall fell down flat, so that the people went up into the city, every man straight before him, and they captured the city. Then they devoted all in the city to destruction, both men and women, young and old, oxen, sheep, and donkeys, with the edge of the sword.

But to the two men who had spied out the land, Joshua said, "Go into the prostitute's house and bring out from there the woman and all who belong to her, as you swore to her." So the young men who had been spies went in and brought out Rahab and her father and mother and brothers and all who belonged to her. And they brought all her relatives and put them outside the camp of Israel. And they burned the city with fire, and everything in it. Only the silver and gold, and the vessels of bronze and of iron, they put into the treasury of the house of the LORD. But Rahab the prostitute and her father's household and all who belonged to her, Joshua saved alive. And she has lived in Israel to this day, because she hid the messengers whom Joshua sent to spy out Jericho (6:12-25).

On the seventh day, the people of Israel marched around the city seven times and then, as God commanded, the priests blew the trumpets and the people gave a loud shout. At the sound of that shout, the walls of the city collapsed and the Israelites entered Jericho unopposed, conquering the city in the name of the Lord.

Joshua honored the promise the spies had made to Rahab. She and her household were spared, but the Israelites burned the city and everything in it. Nothing was left but a layer of ash and blackened debris, which is exactly what archaeologist John Garstang found when he excavated the site in the 1930s.

After the destruction of the city, Joshua made a pronouncement:

Joshua laid an oath on them at that time, saying, "Cursed before the LORD be the man who rises up and rebuilds this city, Jericho.

"At the cost of his firstborn shall he
        lay its foundation,

> and at the cost of his youngest son
>   shall he set up its gates."
> So the LORD was with Joshua, and his fame was in all
> the land (6:26-27).

You may wonder, if Joshua made such an oath, why does the town of Jericho still exist on the West Bank today? The answer is found in the book of 1 Kings. There we read: "In his days Hiel of Bethel built Jericho. He laid its foundation at the cost of Abiram his firstborn, and set up its gates at the cost of his youngest son Segub, according to the word of the LORD, which he spoke by Joshua the son of Nun" (1 Kings 16:34).

Hiel of Bethel pursued his own program and rebuilt Jericho according to his own selfish will—and he and his sons paid the price. Yet God in his sovereign wisdom took the city of Jericho and transformed it into a symbol of his grace. I'm sure you remember the Lord's parable of the Good Samaritan. Jesus began the story by saying, "A man was going down from Jerusalem to Jericho, and he fell among robbers" (Luke 10:30b). In this story, the road to Jericho becomes a place where the words "love your neighbor" are demonstrated in a practical, tangible way.

Later in Luke's gospel, we see Jesus entering Jericho, where he encounters a despised but wealthy tax collector named Zacchaeus. Jesus reaches out to this notorious sinner and transforms his life, prompting Zacchaeus to exclaim, "Behold, Lord, the half of my goods I give to the poor. And if I have defrauded anyone of anything, I restore it fourfold." Jesus replies, "Today salvation has come to this house...For the Son of Man came to seek and to save the lost" (Luke 19:8-10).

Do you see what happened in this account? Yehoshua-Jesus brought salvation to the very city where Yehoshua-Joshua brought destruction! Jericho is also the place where Jesus healed several blind men, including Bartimaeus (see Matthew 20:29-34; Mark 10:46-52; and Luke 18:35-43). The fortress of fear became holy ground—a place where the healing grace of Jesus was poured out on hurting souls.

May we pattern our lives after Jesus and Joshua. Instead of pursuing our own program, then asking God to bless our plans, let's get with God's program. When we obediently submit ourselves to his program and carry out his strategy, he will banish our fears, give us the victory, and make us Christlike agents of his healing grace.

6

The Lessons of Defeat

Joshua 7–8

How much damage can one traitor do?

During the Cold War, a traitor named Clyde Lee Conrad came close to single-handedly causing the nuclear destruction of the free world. Conrad was a retired US Army sergeant living in Germany who sold top-secret information to Soviet spies in the 1970s and 1980s. He also recruited other army retirees and enlisted men, paying them for classified information that he resold at a profit to the Soviets.

Conrad's most damaging betrayal was the sale of the General Defense Plan, NATO's top-secret plans for responding to a Soviet attack. The Plan described in precise detail exactly what the United States and NATO would do if the Soviets invaded Western Europe—where military units would be positioned, NATO's strengths and weaknesses, and more. It was the free world's entire game plan for World War III.

He was arrested in 1988 and convicted of espionage and treason in 1990. Sentenced to life in prison, he died of a heart attack in 1998 while confined in a German prison. He was fifty years old.

The German judge who presided over Conrad's trial described how this one man's crime could have led to utter defeat for the West and millions of deaths in a nuclear holocaust. "If war had broken out between NATO and the Warsaw Pact," the judge concluded, "the West would have faced certain defeat. NATO would have quickly been forced to choose between capitulation or the use of nuclear weapons on German territory. Conrad's treason had doomed the Federal Republic [West Germany] to become a nuclear battlefield."[8]

So how much damage can one traitor do? He can bring his entire nation down in defeat. It happened in Joshua's era, in a place called Ai.

We now come to one of the most heartbreaking sections of the book of Joshua. The people of Israel have just entered the Promised Land. Through faith in the power of God, they have won an amazing victory over Jericho. But immediately after this thrilling triumph the nation of Israel suffers a devastating setback—and the cause of this setback is the moral and spiritual weakness of one man. His actions result in death and defeat for his nation, shame for his family, and the tragic end of his own life.

This is the story of how God's people were betrayed from within and ambushed from without.

The ambush at Ai

Few experiences are more emotionally devastating than being ambushed or betrayed. You are going about your life, unaware of any threat, when sudden disaster strikes. You feel as if a trapdoor has opened beneath your feet. You learn that for weeks or months, while you thought life was going along smoothly, someone you counted on has been betraying you, deceiving you, ruining your reputation, or undermining the foundation of your life.

Out of the blue, your spouse tells you, "I'm leaving you. I want a divorce."

Or you learn that your spouse has been unfaithful to you.

Or your business partner is arrested, and you discover he has been secretly, systematically plundering the company you've been building for years.

Or your teenager gives you the shocking news, "I'm pregnant." Or "I'm addicted to drugs." Or "I don't believe in God anymore."

You cry out, "Why, Lord? Why is this happening?" You've been ambushed. You've gone from victory to a sudden calamity. That's what happened to the people of Israel after the victory at Jericho, when they went up against the city of Ai.

The catastrophe at Ai, recorded in Joshua 7, is foreshadowed in Joshua 6, shortly before the conquest of Jericho begins. There, Joshua tells the Israelites what they should do with any "devoted things," objects of silver and gold that the Canaanites used in their pagan religious ceremonies:

> "But you, keep yourselves from the things devoted to destruction, lest when you have devoted them you take any of the devoted things and make the camp of Israel a thing for destruction and bring trouble upon it. But all silver and gold, and every vessel of bronze and iron, are holy to the LORD; they shall go into the treasury of the LORD" (6:18-19).

After that foreshadowing, we come to Joshua 7 and encounter these ominous words:

> But the people of Israel broke faith in regard to the devoted things, for Achan the son of Carmi, son of Zabdi,

son of Zerah, of the tribe of Judah, took some of the devoted things. And the anger of the LORD burned against the people of Israel (7:1).

Who broke faith with the Lord? "The people of Israel," the Scriptures tell us. How many Israelites were involved in the theft of the devoted objects? One man, "Achan the son of Carmi, son of Zabdi, son of Zerah, of the tribe of Judah." One man committed a sin that would prove destructive to the entire nation.

The account goes on to tell us that Joshua sent spies into Ai, just as he had sent spies into Jericho:

Joshua sent men from Jericho to Ai, which is near Beth-aven, east of Bethel, and said to them, "Go up and spy out the land." And the men went up and spied out Ai. And they returned to Joshua and said to him, "Do not have all the people go up, but let about two or three thousand men go up and attack Ai. Do not make the whole people toil up there, for they are few" (7:2-3).

The spies returned with a glowing report. The city of Ai would be a pushover, even for a small force of two or three thousand soldiers. The battle should have gone exactly as the spies predicted—but something went terribly wrong:

So about three thousand men went up there from the people. And they fled before the men of Ai, and the men of Ai killed about thirty-six of their men and chased them before the gate as far as Shebarim and struck them at the descent. And the hearts of the people melted and became as water.

Then Joshua tore his clothes and fell to the earth on his face before the ark of the LORD until the evening, he and the elders of Israel. And they put dust on their heads. And Joshua said, "Alas, O Lord GOD, why have you brought this people over the Jordan at all, to give us into the hands of the Amorites, to destroy us? Would that we had been content to dwell beyond the Jordan! O Lord, what can I say, when Israel has turned their backs before their enemies! For the Canaanites and all the inhabitants of the land will hear of it and will surround us and cut off our name from the earth. And what will you do for your great name?"(7:4-5).

Joshua tore his clothes and fell upon his face before the ark, asking God why he had allowed Israel to enter this land only to be defeated by the Amorites of Ai. Now all the tribes throughout Canaan would hear of Israel's defeat and would wipe Israel off the map. In response, God told Joshua to stand up, and then he explained to Joshua the reason for Israel's ambush and defeat:

The LORD said to Joshua, "Get up! Why have you fallen on your face? Israel has sinned; they have transgressed my covenant that I commanded them; they have taken some of the devoted things; they have stolen and lied and put them among their own belongings. Therefore the people of Israel cannot stand before their enemies. They turn their backs before their enemies, because they have become devoted for destruction. I will be with you no more, unless you destroy the devoted things from among you. Get up! Consecrate the people and say, 'Consecrate yourselves for tomorrow; for thus says the LORD, God of Israel, "There are devoted things in your midst, O Israel. You cannot stand before your enemies until you take away the devoted things from among you." In the morning therefore you shall be brought near by your tribes. And the tribe that the LORD takes by lot shall come near by clans. And the clan that the LORD takes shall come near by households. And the household that the LORD takes shall come near man by man. And he who is taken with the devoted things shall be burned with fire, he and all that he has, because he has transgressed the covenant of the LORD, and because he has done an outrageous thing in Israel'" (7:10-15).

God doesn't want Joshua's groveling. He wants Joshua to take action and cleanse the people. And the Lord proceeds to tell Joshua how to reconsecrate the people—tribe by tribe, clan by clan, household by household, and man by man. So Joshua does as the Lord commands:

> So Joshua rose early in the morning and brought Israel near tribe by tribe, and the tribe of Judah was taken. And he brought near the clans of Judah, and the clan of the Zerahites was taken. And he brought near the clan of the Zerahites man by man, and Zabdi was taken. And he brought near his household man by man, and Achan the son of Carmi, son of Zabdi, son of Zerah, of the tribe of Judah, was taken. Then Joshua said to Achan, "My son, give glory to the LORD God of Israel and give praise to him. And tell me now what you have done; do not hide it from me." And Achan answered Joshua, "Truly I have sinned against the LORD God of Israel, and this is what I did: when I saw among the spoil a beautiful cloak from Shinar, and 200 shekels of silver, and a bar of gold weighing 50 shekels, then I coveted them and took them. And see, they are hidden in the earth inside my tent, with the silver underneath" (7:16-21).

Through a divine process of elimination, the perpetrator of the theft is revealed, and the perpetrator, Achan, confesses his sin. He is the one who, through disobedience to God, betrayed the nation by taking and hiding some of the plunder from Jericho. Here's what happened next:

So Joshua sent messengers, and they ran to the tent; and behold, it was hidden in his tent with the silver underneath. And they took them out of the tent and brought them to Joshua and to all the people of Israel. And they laid them down before the LORD. And Joshua and all Israel with him took Achan the son of Zerah, and the silver and the cloak and the bar of gold, and his sons and daughters and his oxen and donkeys and sheep and his tent and all that he had. And they brought them up to the Valley of Achor. And Joshua said, "Why did you bring trouble on us? The LORD brings trouble on you today." And all Israel stoned him with stones. They burned them with fire and stoned them with stones. And they raised over him a great heap of stones that remains to this day. Then the LORD turned from his burning anger. Therefore, to this day the name of that place is called the Valley of Achor (7:22-26).

It's a grim ending to a tragic and instructive story. Joshua sends messengers to search Achan's tent. They bring out the stolen items and spread them on the ground before the people, in the sight of the Lord. The penalty is death—execution by stoning. This may seem like an extreme penalty for pilfering some plunder from the conquest of Jericho. But is it? All the people of Israel had been warned. Because of his actions, thirty-six brave Hebrew warriors had died in battle. Their blood was on Achan's hands.

So Achan was executed by stoning and his body was burned. Everything he owned was destroyed in a place called the Valley of Achor (the Hebrew word *achor* means "trouble"). A large pile of rocks was erected over the site of Achan's execution.

Responding to trials and tragedy

Some people look at Bible passages like this one and draw the conclusion that when bad things happen to believers, it must be a judgment from God. That's not always true. Trials and tragedies are a natural part of living in a fallen world. God's people sometimes suffer through no fault of their own.

True, God *sometimes* uses adversity in our lives to make us aware of our need for change. Suffering can be a consequence of sin. When we encounter a trial of adversity, we need to examine our lives and ask ourselves, *Is God trying to get my attention? Are these problems the result of sin in my life?* And we need to ask God, *What are you trying to teach me? I don't want to miss any of the lessons you have for me, so please help me understand what you are saying to me through this trial.*

When Israel suffered a setback at Ai, Joshua immediately cast himself down before God in prayer. He wanted to understand the reason for this setback. He wanted to root out the sin that had caused death and defeat for his people. So, together with the elders of the nation of Israel, he went before God and sought an answer.

How different Joshua's response was from the way you and I often react to defeat or loss: "God, it's not fair! I shouldn't have to suffer like this!" We often rationalize our sins and refuse to give them up. We resist God as he tugs at our conscience. We sweep our dirty secrets under the rug instead of allowing God to clean house.

Remember what Joshua said when he fell on his face before God: "Alas, O Lord GOD, why have you brought this people over the Jordan at all, to give us into the hands of the Amorites, to destroy us?" It was commendable for Joshua to go to God with his questions—but do you not detect a note of accusation in that question? Joshua is saying, in effect, "Lord, how could you do that to us? You've let us down! Did you bring us all this way just to hand us over to our enemies? Lord, you owe us an explanation!"

This is a very human response on Joshua's part. It is often our nature to question God. I have done so. I'm sure you have as well.

We think that God has let us down, and we blame him for our troubles.

But God had not let Israel down. The nation was betrayed from within. Someone in the camp broke the covenant. Someone disobeyed God's injunction. Someone stole what belonged to God. The result of disobedience was defeat—not merely for one man but for the nation. Innocent men died and the battle was lost because of one man's hidden sin.

It's important to understand that the seeds of Israel's defeat at Ai were planted at the very moment of Israel's triumph over Jericho. This is a scenario we can all relate to as Christians. When we struggle with problems in our lives, when we face rivers of impossibility and fortresses of fear, we recognize our need of God. We purge sin from our lives and earnestly seek to obey God's will.

So God in his mercy answers our prayers. He delivers us and leads us in triumph through our adversity. We are ecstatic, joyful, and grateful to God—*for a while*.

But that euphoric sense of gratitude doesn't last long. We become comfortable and a little smug. Things are going well now. We think we don't need God's help at the moment. We think we don't need to pray as much as we once did. And if we start returning to those former bad habits, we figure God will understand and overlook it.

Perhaps that was the attitude of Achan. He had marched with the army of Israel and had seen the walls of Jericho destroyed by a trumpet blast and a shout. That was the moment of Israel's triumph. Achan was overjoyed and grateful to God.

But as Achan plundered one of the Canaanite storehouses, something caught his eye. He saw a beautiful robe from Babylonia, two hundred shekels of shining silver, and a gleaming wedge of gold. In the moment of Israel's triumph, he coveted the things that belonged to God. At the moment of victory, Achan stole and ensured future defeat.

Perhaps you identify with Achan. Perhaps you have lost touch with God, and sins that were once unthinkable have become habitual. Perhaps you are withholding the tithe that belongs to the Lord. Then it happens: You experience a defeat, an ambush. Like Joshua, you find yourself crying out, "Why, Lord? Why is this happening to me?"

Defeat does not have to be the end of your story. You have fallen, but God wants to lift you up. You've been sidelined, but God wants to restore you to usefulness for him. There are at least three stages to every experience of defeat and restoration. These stages follow each other as day follows night. The stages are:

Step 1: Carelessness
Step 2: Calamity
Step 3: Closure

Let's look at each stage.

Step 1: Carelessness

One of our greatest dangers as Christians is that we underestimate the power of sin. We say, "I know what the Bible says about sin—but that doesn't apply to my situation. I'm saved by God's grace. Jesus died on the cross for my sins and I have liberty in him. Oh, I know I shouldn't do some of the things I do, but God in his grace overlooks my sins. I'm not worried about consequences."

Underneath this lax attitude toward sin is a burning, raging conscience. Though we may rationalize our disobedience, we know deep down that God does not overlook sin. We may be careless about sin, but God never is—and only a fool takes God's grace for granted. That's why the Scriptures tell us, "work out your own salvation with fear and trembling" (Philippians 2:12b). The sin of disobedience is serious, but equally serious is the sin of presumption. We should never take the grace and mercy of God for granted. Our attitude toward God's grace should be one of grateful obedience, not presumptuous sin. We rationalize our disobedience and presume upon God's grace in several ways.

Disobedience in our finances. We are quick to rationalize a choice to spend God's tithes on ourselves. According to George Barna, founder of the Barna Group, tithing has become "uncommon" in churches today. He writes, "For a number of years, The Barna Group has…been following the practice of 'tithing,' which is donating at least ten percent of one's income…Very few Americans tithed in 2004. Only 4 percent gave such an amount to churches alone; just 6 percent gave to either churches or to a combination of churches and parachurch ministries."[9]

Understand, those dismal numbers were reported in 2004, during a wildly optimistic economic boom. After the economic downturn of 2008, tithing took a nosedive. In November 2008, 22 percent of Americans said they had completely stopped giving to the church; another 52 percent had sharply reduced their giving; in April 2011, 24 percent completely stopped giving.[10] The tithe belongs to the Lord, and he has commanded that we bring our tithes and offerings into his storehouse. It is a tragedy that Christians today are woefully disobedient in the use of their finances.

Disobedience in our ethical behavior. Your integrity and ethical behavior are essential to your witness in this sinful world. If your behavior as a Christian conforms to the behavior of the world, what difference does it make to be a Christian? What example do you set for the people around you that would stir their hunger to know Jesus?

Many Christians explain away their unethical behavior, saying, "You have to cut a few corners to compete in the business world today. Integrity is old-fashioned. In today's economy, you do what it takes to survive." Well, I won't kid you. Sometimes you pay a price to maintain your integrity. Maintaining your Christian ethical standards could cost you a sale—or even your career. But your willingness to maintain your integrity at any cost will give you a powerful testimony for Jesus Christ.

I once had a conversation with a brilliant young Christian businessman. He had been with his company for fourteen years and was highly regarded in his field. But he had reached an invisible ceiling and was stuck there, unable to obtain a promotion. When he asked his superiors why other, less qualified people were being promoted ahead of him, they told him he needed to be patient.

Finally, one of his coworkers told him that the word around the office was that he was kept out of management because he wouldn't lie or cheat the customer. His integrity had blocked his advancement in the company. "That hurt," he told me, "but I had the consolation of knowing I had built a reputation for honesty. I'll probably never get promoted, but at least I know I am a witness in the office."

Integrity isn't cheap, but it's worth every cent it costs you. If you are willing to trade your integrity for money and status, I pity you. As Jesus said, "For what does it profit a man to gain the whole world and forfeit his soul?" (Mark 8:36).

Disobedience in our sexual and moral behavior. King David stood on his rooftop and saw a beautiful woman bathing below. He could have turned away—but he stayed, he looked, and he lusted. That moment of lust led to his undoing. He followed the urgings of his flesh into the depths of adultery and murder. He arranged for the death of another man and took that man's wife as his own.

When David's sin was revealed, God, speaking through the prophet Nathan, told him, "Now therefore the sword shall never depart from your house, because you have despised me and have taken the wife of Uriah the Hittite to be your wife" (2 Samuel 12:10). This prediction was fulfilled when David's own beloved son Absalom led a revolt against David and plunged Israel into civil war. And it all began with a moment of lust.

What thoughts occupy the secret places of your mind? How do you use your computer when no one else is looking? What kinds of programs do you watch on television? What kinds of movies do you view? What kinds of books do you read? What kinds of thoughts do you have about other people in your neighborhood, at your office, or on your campus? Do you think about how to reach them for Christ—or would you be ashamed if your thoughts were revealed to the world?

We must no longer rationalize our disobedience or take God's grace for granted. God does not overlook sin, and neither should we. You may be able to rationalize sin for a while, but sooner or later the consequences will catch up to you.

The carelessness of Achan

You may think, *It's just a little sin. Who does it hurt?* Yet it was just a little bite from the forbidden fruit that doomed Adam's race to death. And it was just a robe, a few pieces of silver, and a bar of gold that Achan stole, yet it cost Israel the victory at Ai. Sin is like a pebble cast into a pond, and you never know how far the ripples will spread. As the seventeenth-century English preacher Jeremiah Burroughs warned, "Take heed of secret sins. They will undo thee if loved and maintained: one moth may spoil the garment; one leak drown the ship…Therefore take heed that secret sinnings eat not out good beginnings."[11]

Who was this man Achan? Can we dismiss him as nothing more than a thief with a lust for silver and gold? Or is he more like us than we would like to admit? Perhaps he stole because he was fearful and insecure, and he thought that possessing a few items of silver and gold would enable him to build a secure future for himself and his family. We should ask ourselves, *In what ways am I like Achan? What can I learn from his story?*

Remember what we learned in the previous chapter: Fear and faith are like the two ends of a seesaw. When fear is up, faith is down. When faith is up, fear is down. I think Achan was probably a fearful man. He felt insecure about the future. He didn't trust in the constancy of God's provision. He worried about whether he would have enough money to provide for his family.

Achan's level of fear was high, so his level of faith was low. At the moment of Israel's triumph in Jericho, Achan was unable to trust in God's provision. Even though God had provided manna for the Israelites to eat during their forty years in the wilderness, Achan did not trust God to provide. Even though God had enabled Israel to cross the river of impossibility, Achan did not trust God to deliver.

It was as if Achan were saying, "Yes, I know of all the great things God has done in the past, but how do I know he will continue to do great things in the future? What if he forgets us? How do I know I can trust God in the future?" That is deadly thinking. If you doubt God's loving provision in the future, then you do not trust the faithfulness of God. Your fear will lead you to rationalize sin. Achan's fearfulness led him to become careless about sin—and his carelessness led him to *calamity*.

Step 2: Calamity

Achan's careless disobedience brought disaster to himself, his family, and his nation. We think our secret sins affect no one else. We think we can hoard our tithes and offerings and it won't matter to God or to the church. We think, *God doesn't need my money*. And that's true, he doesn't. But we need to give! God tells us in his Word:

> "Will man rob God? Yet you are robbing me. But you say, 'How have we robbed you?' In your tithes and contributions. You are cursed with a curse, for you are robbing me, the whole nation of you. Bring the full tithe into the storehouse, that there may be food in my house. And thereby put me to the test, says the LORD of hosts, if I will not open the windows of heaven for you and pour down for you a blessing until there is no more need" (Malachi 3:8-10).

You might think, *Well, Michael Youssef is just trying to manipulate people into giving money to the church.* I assure you, I talk about this subject only because I'm committed to teaching everything in God's Word. God says that those who withhold the tithe are robbing him, so if you carry this principle to its logical conclusion, then people who withhold their tithe from God are driving to church in stolen cars, sitting in church wearing stolen clothes, and sitting down to a Sunday supper of stolen food.

God will be patient with us for a while, but only for a while. And when his patience comes to an end—*calamity*! When we cry out to God in the midst of our calamity, he will say to us, "Remember what I told you in my Word. Carelessness leads to calamity."

God wants us to go from one glorious victory to the next, from one height to an even greater height, from one mountaintop to an even higher mountaintop. He takes no pleasure in our setbacks and defeats. Calamity is not his will for our lives.

He is pleased to use us to touch the lives of others. He places others in our path so that we will reach out to them and share the good news of Jesus Christ with them. In the process, we will ultimately claim our neighborhood, our workplace, or our school for Jesus Christ one life at a time. My friend, do not be careless with sin, for carelessness leads to calamity, and calamity will mar your testimony. Purge the hidden sin from your life and keep your witness for Christ pure and untarnished.

Do that, and you will be ready for *closure*.

Step 3. Closure

In Book VIII of his *Confessions*, Augustine wrote these words, admitting his guilt before God: "At the beginning of my youth, I begged you to make me virtuous, and I said, 'Give me chastity and self-control—only not yet.' For I feared that you would hear me too soon, and that you would quickly cure me of the disease of my sinful desires. I wanted to satisfy those desires, not extinguish them" (my paraphrase).

Perhaps you can identify with Augustine's confessions. Perhaps you have wanted to satisfy your sinful desires, not extinguish them. You know those sins are wrong and they are dangerous to you and to the people around you. You would like God to purge those sins from your life—but not yet. You want to enjoy them a little longer.

So you say, "Lord, I definitely plan to get rid of those sins— someday. But there's no need to rush things." That is an attitude of carelessness toward sin, and it keeps you from being an effective witness for Christ. It keeps you from experiencing victory in your life. It is an Achan-like attitude that will lead you to calamity unless you find the closure God wants you to experience.

What kind of closure am I talking about? *Repentance*. To repent is to turn to God and say, "Lord, I want to be fully obedient to you. I want you to take all the hidden sin out of my life—not someday, but now. Lord, I turn from my sin. I choose full obedience to you. Seal this commitment and give me the power to keep it."

Don't think you can repent of your sin once and for all, and you will never be tempted again. *You will be tempted.* You may fail a time or two. But God knows if your desire to repent is sincere. When you fall, he will lift you up and say, "Try again, child."

In the Old Testament book of Hosea, there's an amazing passage where God speaks of Israel as an adulterous wife who has betrayed the marriage covenant:

> "And I will punish her for the feast days of the Baals
>   when she burned offerings to them
> and adorned herself with her ring and jewelry,
>   and went after her lovers
>   and forgot me, declares the LORD."
> (Hosea 2:13)

At first glance, the Lord's words seem angry. He speaks of punishing Israel for her infidelity. But then he goes on to declare his gracious love for Israel:

> "Therefore, behold, I will allure her,
>   and bring her into the wilderness,
>   and speak tenderly to her.
> And there I will give her her vineyards
>   and make the Valley of Achor a door of hope.
> And there she shall answer as in the days of her youth,
>   as at the time when she came out of the land of Egypt."
> (Hosea 2:14-15)

God says he will make the Valley of Achor a door of hope. What is the Valley of Achor? It's the place where Achan was executed by stoning! And God, through the prophet Hosea, tells us that this place where Achan confessed his sin, then paid the consequences of his sin, shall become a door of hope.

When we confess our sins and purge disobedience from our lives, we pass through a door of hope. We experience a new beginning in our lives and a new life of faithfulness to God.

A new chapter

Once you have cleansed your life from hidden sin, prepare yourself for the victory God gives you. Walk through the door of hope that opens before you. Israel was defeated at Ai because of Achan's sin. But the defeat at Ai was not the end of Israel's story. After the sin was purged, God wrote a new chapter in the story of Israel. Joshua 7 is the story of Achan's sin and Israel's defeat—but then comes Joshua 8:

> And the LORD said to Joshua, "Do not fear and do not be dismayed. Take all the fighting men with you, and arise, go up to Ai. See, I have given into your hand the king of Ai, and his people, his city, and his land. And you shall do to Ai and its king as you did to Jericho and its king. Only its spoil and its livestock you shall take as plunder for yourselves. Lay an ambush against the city, behind it."
>
> So Joshua and all the fighting men arose to go up to Ai. And Joshua chose 30,000 mighty men of valor and sent them out by night. And he commanded them, "Behold, you shall lie in ambush against the city, behind it. Do not go very far from the city, but all of you remain ready. And I and all the people who are with me will approach the city. And when they come out against us just as before, we shall flee before them. And they will come out after us, until we have drawn them away from the city. For they will say, 'They are fleeing from us, just as before.' So we will flee before them. Then you shall rise up from the

ambush and seize the city, for the LORD your God will give it into your hand. And as soon as you have taken the city, you shall set the city on fire. You shall do according to the word of the LORD. See, I have commanded you." So Joshua sent them out. And they went to the place of ambush and lay between Bethel and Ai, to the west of Ai, but Joshua spent that night among the people.

Joshua arose early in the morning and mustered the people and went up, he and the elders of Israel, before the people to Ai. And all the fighting men who were with him went up and drew near before the city and encamped on the north side of Ai, with a ravine between them and Ai. He took about 5,000 men and set them in ambush between Bethel and Ai, to the west of the city. So they stationed the forces, the main encampment that was north of the city and its rear guard west of the city. But Joshua spent that night in the valley. And as soon as the king of Ai saw this, he and all his people, the men of the city, hurried and went out early to the appointed place toward the Arabah to meet Israel in battle. But he did not know that there was an ambush against him behind the city. And Joshua and all Israel pretended to be beaten before them and fled in the direction of the wilderness. So all the people who were in the city were called together to pursue them, and as they pursued Joshua they were drawn away from the city. Not a man was left in Ai or Bethel who did not go out after Israel. They left the city open and pursued Israel.

Then the LORD said to Joshua, "Stretch out the javelin that is in your hand toward Ai, for I will give it into your hand." And Joshua stretched out the javelin that was in his hand toward the city. And the men in the ambush rose quickly out of their place, and as soon as he had stretched out his hand, they ran and entered the city and captured it.

And they hurried to set the city on fire. So when the men of Ai looked back, behold, the smoke of the city went up to heaven, and they had no power to flee this way or that, for the people who fled to the wilderness turned back against the pursuers. And when Joshua and all Israel saw that the ambush had captured the city, and that the smoke of the city went up, then they turned back and struck down the men of Ai. And the others came out from the city against them, so they were in the midst of Israel, some on this side, and some on that side. And Israel struck them down, until there was left none that survived or escaped. But the king of Ai they took alive, and brought him near to Joshua.

When Israel had finished killing all the inhabitants of Ai in the open wilderness where they pursued them, and all of them to the very last had fallen by the edge of the sword, all Israel returned to Ai and struck it down with the edge of the sword. And all who fell that day, both men and women, were 12,000, all the people of Ai. But Joshua did not draw back his hand with which he stretched out the javelin until he had devoted all the inhabitants of Ai to destruction. Only the livestock and the spoil of that city Israel took as their plunder, according to the word of the LORD that he commanded Joshua. So Joshua burned Ai and made it forever a heap of ruins, as it is to this day. And he hanged the king of Ai on a tree until evening. And at sunset Joshua commanded, and they took his body down from the tree and threw it at the entrance of the gate of the city and raised over it a great heap of stones, which stands there to this day (8:1-29).

At God's command, Joshua and the army of Israel ambushed the army of Ai, conquered the city, and killed the pagan inhabitants of the city—about 12,000 men and women. Now, you probably find such wholesale slaughter disturbing. Though this story doesn't make me doubt the goodness of God or the justice of his judgment, one can't help feeling compassion and sadness for those who were put to the sword.

Atheists and so-called freethinkers like to use incidents such as this one to portray God as bloodthirsty and genocidal. They ignore God's explanation of his reasons for commanding Joshua and the Israelites to conquer these cities and eliminate their populations. We will examine God's reasons in greater depth in chapter 8, but for now it's worth noting that the Canaanite people engaged in horrifying idolatrous practices, including sacrificing their own children to their demon gods. Imagine parents tossing their own babies alive into the fires or suffocating them in funerary jars!

Speaking through Moses, God explained why these pagan cultures had to be destroyed:

> "When the LORD your God brings you into the land that you are entering to take possession of it, and clears away many nations before you, the Hittites, the Girgashites, the Amorites, the Canaanites, the Perizzites, the Hivites, and the Jebusites, seven nations more numerous and mightier than you, and when the LORD your God gives them over to you, and you defeat them, then you must devote them to complete destruction. You shall make no covenant with them and show no mercy to them. You shall not intermarry with them, giving your daughters to their sons or taking their daughters for your sons, for they would turn away your sons from following me, to serve other gods. Then the anger of the LORD would be kindled against you, and he would destroy you quickly" (Deuteronomy 7:1-4).

God chose the people of Israel as the means of one day bringing the Messiah into the world. He wanted to keep the people of Israel

morally and spiritually pure. He knew that if the various Canaanite tribes were permitted to live, the Jewish people would never be
free from the moral and spiritual corruption of Canaanite idolatry.
God warned the people of Israel that if they did not obey his command and destroy the Canaanite people, their sons and daughters
would intermarry with them, and they would be turned away from
God to serve other gods.

Though these measures may seem extreme today, it's important
that we put ourselves in the sandals of Joshua and his people. They
were surrounded by enemies who would destroy them physically,
morally, and spiritually if given the chance. The survival of the Jewish people and the lineage of the Messiah depended on Israel's obedience to these stern commands.

After the conquest of Ai, Joshua addressed the spiritual needs of
the people of Israel. The Scriptures tell us:

> At that time Joshua built an altar to the LORD, the God
> of Israel, on Mount Ebal, just as Moses the servant of the
> LORD had commanded the people of Israel, as it is written
> in the Book of the Law of Moses, "an altar of uncut stones,
> upon which no man has wielded an iron tool." And they
> offered on it burnt offerings to the LORD and sacrificed
> peace offerings. And there, in the presence of the peo-
> ple of Israel, he wrote on the stones a copy of the law of
> Moses, which he had written. And all Israel, sojourner
> as well as native born, with their elders and officers and
> their judges, stood on opposite sides of the ark before the
> Levitical priests who carried the ark of the covenant of the
> LORD, half of them in front of Mount Gerizim and half of
> them in front of Mount Ebal, just as Moses the servant of
> the LORD had commanded at the first, to bless the people
> of Israel. And afterward he read all the words of the law,
> the blessing and the curse, according to all that is written

in the Book of the Law. There was not a word of all that
Moses commanded that Joshua did not read before all the
assembly of Israel, and the women, and the little ones, and
the sojourners who lived among them (8:30-35).

Joshua built an altar to the God of Israel on Mount Ebal, and he
offered sacrifices upon the altar. There he read the words of the Law
of Moses before all the assembled people of Israel, and Israel reaffirmed its covenant with the Lord.

Don't ignore the warning signs

A few years ago, my brother went to be with the Lord at the age
of sixty-eight. He was a brilliant economist and one of the godliest men I've ever known. He was instrumental in leading me to the
Lord. I love him and miss him dearly.

Two years before his death, I learned that he'd been having physical symptoms that sounded like the warning signs of colon cancer.
Knowing him as I do, I pleaded with him to get medical attention,
but he refused to see a doctor. By the time the symptoms became
so serious he could no longer ignore them, the cancer had spread
throughout his body. His condition was terminal.

My friend, please do not ignore the warning signs. Do not dismiss the symptoms. Disobedience to God is a deadly spiritual cancer. Don't rationalize the hidden sin eating away at your spiritual
life and your relationship with God. While you ignore the symptoms, the disease of sin continues its deadly progression. Purge this
malignancy from your life before it robs you of your spiritual vitality.

Carelessness with sin leads to calamity, just as the carelessness of
Achan led to defeat at Ai. But like Israel, we can move from calamity to closure by repenting of our sin and purging it from our lives.
Once we have moved to closure with God, we can step through the
door of hope and walk through the gates of victory.

7

God's Wisdom for Difficult Decisions

Joshua 9

I once spoke with a group of young Christian professional people in the Middle East. We discussed some of the challenges they faced in the business world, and one of them said, "In business, lying is so commonplace that you can never know for sure whether someone is telling the truth." Others nodded agreement.

I turned to a young professional woman in the group and asked, "Don't business relationships depend on trust? A contract or verbal agreement means nothing if you can't trust the other person's word. How can you do business in such an environment?"

"I constantly pray for discernment and wisdom," she replied.

You may say, "Well, that problem is unique to a certain culture in a distant land. Here in America, we have a different view of honesty and integrity. And while we've had our share of business and political scandals, we can generally trust one another. The one place we need not worry about being deceived is the church in America."

If that is your view, let me share some sobering facts. During a four-year period in the United States, churchgoing folks were bilked out of $450 million by scam artists who posed as church members. These con men joined the church and became functioning members of the congregation. They spoke the Christian language. They could recite Scripture and pray like any real believer. They played their parts well—but they cheated churchgoers out of their life savings through phony investment schemes. They preyed upon the trust that Christians naturally have for one another in the body of Christ.

Some years ago, a man wept bitter tears in my office. He was the son of a pastor in a major Christian denomination, yet he was facing prison time for using his position of trust in the church to defraud scores of ministers. He had convinced these pastors to place their retirement funds in a bogus investment program. He raked in hundreds of thousands of dollars, the life savings of these Christian leaders—and the money evaporated. He said he was sorry and he cried real tears, but it was too late.

I had to ask myself, *How had so many Christian ministers been taken in by this scheme? Pastors are supposed to be people of maturity and discernment. They are shepherds of their flocks, yet they themselves had been sheared like sheep! Had any of them prayed for wisdom and discernment before handing their life savings over to this con man?*

Deceivers are all around us. We Christians seem to be especially susceptible to their schemes precisely because of our desire to build trusting relationships based on biblical principles of *koinonia* fellowship. But there is no virtue in being gullible. Again and again, in both the Old and the New Testaments, God tells his people to be wise and to not be deceived.

We are about to see how even such a wise leader as Joshua could be duped. Whenever we face a key decision in our lives, our first response must be to pray for wisdom and discernment.

The scheme of the Gibeonites

As Joshua 9 opens, word of Israel's victories over Jericho and Ai has spread far and wide, from the hill country to the low country to the Mediterranean coast:

> As soon as all the kings who were beyond the Jordan in the hill country and in the lowland all along the coast of the Great Sea toward Lebanon, the Hittites, the Amorites, the Canaanites, the Perizzites, the Hivites, and the Jebusites, heard of this, they gathered together as one to fight against Joshua and Israel (9:1-2).

The pagan kings throughout the land join forces to fend off the Israelite invaders. But the tribe of Gibeon devises a different approach. The Gibeonites concoct a scheme of deception:

> But when the inhabitants of Gibeon heard what Joshua had done to Jericho and to Ai, they on their part acted with cunning and went and made ready provisions and took worn-out sacks for their donkeys, and wineskins, worn-out and torn and mended, with worn-out, patched sandals on their feet, and worn-out clothes. And all their provisions were dry and crumbly. And they went to Joshua in the camp at Gilgal and said to him and to the men of Israel, "We have come from a distant country, so now make a covenant with us." But the men of Israel said to the Hivites, "Perhaps you live among us; then how can we make a covenant with you?" They said to Joshua, "We are your servants." And Joshua said to them, "Who are you? And where do you come from?" They said to him, "From a very

distant country your servants have come, because of the name of the LORD your God. For we have heard a report of him, and all that he did in Egypt, and all that he did to the two kings of the Amorites who were beyond the Jordan, to Sihon the king of Heshbon, and to Og king of Bashan, who lived in Ashtaroth. So our elders and all the inhabitants of our country said to us, 'Take provisions in your hand for the journey and go to meet them and say to them, "We are your servants. Come now, make a covenant with us."' Here is our bread. It was still warm when we took it from our houses as our food for the journey on the day we set out to come to you, but now, behold, it is dry and crumbly. These wineskins were new when we filled them, and behold, they have burst. And these garments and sandals of ours are worn out from the very long journey." So the men took some of their provisions, but did not ask counsel from the LORD. And Joshua made peace with them and made a covenant with them, to let them live, and the leaders of the congregation swore to them (9:3-15).

The saddest statement in that passage is verse 14: "So the men took some of their provisions, *but did not ask counsel from the LORD.*" These words signal trouble ahead.

The deceptive Gibeonites sent a delegation to the Israelite camp at Gilgal. The Gibeonites wore beat-up sandals and threadbare robes and were laden with parched wineskins and patchwork sacks filled with dry, moldy food. They arrived at Gilgal, seemingly a bunch of bedraggled, dusty people in old clothes, with tired-looking donkeys. The Gibeonites lied to Joshua, claiming to come from a distant country, eager to make a peace treaty with Israel—and because Joshua and the elders of Israel failed to ask counsel from the Lord, they took the bait.

Here we see the danger of trusting human wisdom.

Vulnerable to deception

Why did Joshua fail to ask God for wisdom and discernment? If we want to understand the lessons of this story for our lives, we need to place it in context. Joshua's error in judgment didn't happen in a vacuum. There's a reason why he and the elders of Israel were vulnerable to deception—and we find that reason in the previous chapter.

At the end of Joshua 8, the army of Israel has conquered the city of Ai. In gratitude to God, Joshua builds an altar on Mount Ebal. He offers sacrifices, reads the Law of Moses to the people, and reaffirms Israel's covenant with the Lord. In short, Joshua and his people have just experienced a spiritual revival. They have rededicated themselves to God and have pledged obedience to his Word.

The Israelites have gone through a "mountaintop experience"—and mountaintops can be spiritual danger zones. We should always be especially watchful immediately after a spiritual victory. The euphoria of a mountaintop experience can make us vulnerable to spiritual deception. Many sincere Christians have fallen prey to Satan's traps immediately after a spiritual highpoint.

As Paul wrote to the Corinthians, "Therefore let anyone who thinks that he stands take heed lest he fall" (1 Corinthians 10:12). When you think you have it made, watch out! That's precisely when you are most vulnerable to Satan's schemes.

Sometimes a mountaintop experience *literally* takes place on a mountaintop, such as a Christian retreat or conference in the mountains. You spend a few days surrounded by the beauty of God's creation and you listen to Christian speakers who challenge you to a deeper walk with God. You respond, you rededicate your life to Christ, and you come away feeling that you have turned a corner in your Christian experience. You'll never go back to being the person you once were.

But as soon as you return to your everyday life, Satan attacks, hitting you with one temptation after another. Or you experience a series of trials and setbacks. Or you are beset by frustration and opposition. And you wonder, *What happened? When I was on the mountaintop, I felt so close to God. I was on top of the world! My relationship with God was never stronger. Now I'm at the lowest point in my spiritual life. I don't know how it happened.*

Or perhaps you got involved in an outreach program in your community. You've seen God use you in a great way as you've shared your testimony with others. You've been helping to meet human need, sharing your time and resources with the poor and disadvantaged. You feel closer to God than you've ever felt before. And that's when Satan ambushes you! Suddenly, you learn that the Christian leader you looked up to is a fraud. Or you find that your reputation is under attack and your motives are being questioned. Or you find yourself blindsided by intense temptation. You wonder, *Why am I suddenly experiencing problems I've never had before?*

Don't be surprised if you suddenly experience opposition and deception just as you begin to be effective for Jesus Christ. Satan is watching for signs of vulnerability, and he wants to quench God's power in our lives. The moment we begin to breathe deeply of the Spirit of God, Satan will try to smother us.

When Jesus began his messianic ministry of preaching, healing, and casting out demons, he soon faced a barrage of opposition. Three groups that had traditionally quarreled and struggled against one aother suddenly united against their common enemy, Jesus of Nazareth. These groups—the Pharisees, Sadducees, and Herodians—remained united in their hostility toward Jesus throughout his public ministry.

Whenever you become serious about exercising your calling and your apostleship, whenever you speak out for God, whenever you claim your workplace or campus or neighborhood for Christ, expect opposition. The moment you become effective for Christ is the moment all hell breaks loose! That's why you must pray for wisdom and discernment when you are besieged by Satan and his schemes.

An unwise oath

Joshua 9 goes on to tell us that after the Israelites had made a treaty with the Gibeonites, word came that these people didn't live in a distant country after all:

> At the end of three days after they had made a covenant with them, they heard that they were their neighbors and that they lived among them. And the people of Israel set out and reached their cities on the third day. Now their cities were Gibeon, Chephirah, Beeroth, and Kiriath-jearim. But the people of Israel did not attack them, because the leaders of the congregation had sworn to them by the LORD, the God of Israel. Then all the congregation murmured against the leaders. But all the leaders said to all the congregation, "We have sworn to them by the LORD, the God of Israel, and now we may not touch them. This we will do to them: let them live, lest wrath be upon us, because of the oath that we swore to them." And the leaders said to them, "Let them live." So they became cutters of wood and drawers of water for all the congregation, just as the leaders had said of them (9:16-21).

When the leaders of Israel learned they had been fooled, they resolved to honor the oath they had sworn before God, even though the treaty had been based on deception. The people of Israel were understandably displeased with their leaders, but the elders replied that they had not just signed a treaty, *they had sworn a solemn and binding oath* before God. Breaking the oath would bring God's wrath down on them. So the elders decreed that the Gibeonites would live, but would serve the Israelites as woodcutters and water carriers.

Next, Joshua confronted the Gibeonites about their deception:

> Joshua summoned them, and he said to them, "Why did you deceive us, saying, 'We are very far from you,' when you dwell among us? Now therefore you are cursed, and some of you shall never be anything but servants, cutters of wood and drawers of water for the house of my God." They answered Joshua, "Because it was told to your servants for a certainty that the LORD your God had commanded his servant Moses to give you all the land and to destroy all the inhabitants of the land from before you—so we feared greatly for our lives because of you and did this thing. And now, behold, we are in your hand. Whatever seems good and right in your sight to do to us, do it." So he did this to them and delivered them out of the hand of the people of Israel, and they did not kill them. But Joshua made them that day cutters of wood and drawers of water for the congregation and for the altar of the LORD, to this day, in the place that he should choose (9:22-27).

The Gibeonites explained that they had fooled Israel for the sake of self-preservation. They knew God had commanded Moses "to destroy all the inhabitants of the land from before you"—so they reasoned that it was better to lie and live than to tell the truth and die.

The deceptive strategy

If you go to Israel and visit the Arab village of al-Jib, north of Jerusalem, you will be standing on the site of ancient Gibeon. The ancient city was excavated from 1956 to 1962 by James B. Prichard, an archaeologist from the University of Pennsylvania. Pritchard and his team uncovered many structures, wine cellars, water conduits, and artifacts that match the biblical accounts regarding the city of Gibeon. They even excavated a large pool that matches the biblical description of the Pool of Gibeon mentioned in 2 Samuel 2:13. Hebrew inscriptions found in the ruins confirm that the site is that of the biblical city of Gibeon.

So once again, secular archaeology confirms that the Old Testament record is a reliable historical account. The lessons of this biblical text come to us from actual events. And one of the most important insights we can learn from this story is the same one the Lord gave to the prophet Samuel when he was in search of a man to replace Saul, whom the Lord had rejected as king: "But the LORD said to Samuel, 'Do not look on his appearance or on the height of his stature, because I have rejected him. For the LORD sees not as man sees: man looks on the outward appearance, but the LORD looks on the heart'" (1 Samuel 16:7).

That's why we need wisdom and discernment from God. Whenever we face a crucial decision, we need to see the situation from God's perspective, not a merely human perspective. As the New Testament tells us, "If any of you lacks wisdom, let him ask God, who gives generously to all without reproach, and it will be given him" (James 1:5). Notice, the Bible doesn't say that God *may* give you wisdom. It says God *will* give it to you—generously and in abundance. That's a promise from God.

Joshua's vow to the Gibeonites, sealed with an oath before God, will later prove to have tragic consequences for the nation of Israel. In 2 Samuel 21, when Israel endures three years of famine, David asks the Lord why the nation is suffering and starving. God tells David it is because King Saul has slaughtered many of the Gibeonite people in violation of the oath that Joshua had made.

Joshua should not have made that oath—and he would not

have made it had he prayed for discernment. Joshua and the elders looked upon the outward appearance. They failed to ask God what was at the heart of the matter.

The Gibeonites knew that God had commanded the Israelites to invade the land of Canaan and wipe out all the inhabitants. They knew their cities stood directly in the path of the Israelite onslaught and that they couldn't defeat God's people. That's why they resorted to deception. You may ask, "How did the Gibeonites know that God had commanded Israel to wipe out the inhabitants of the land?"

The Scriptures don't tell us how the Gibeonites knew. Somehow word reached them of what God had said to Israel, as recorded in Deuteronomy 20. There, God had told the Israelites that they should wipe out their enemies, plunder the nearby cities, make peace treaties with the distant cities, and take over the Promised Land. The Gibeonites knew God's command to Israel and they quoted it verbatim.

There is a lesson in this account that we can apply to our lives today: Deceivers often know the Bible better than we do. They will use the Scriptures to confuse you, tie you up in knots, and silence you. They'll say, "Doesn't the Bible say that God is love? Then how can you say that a loving God will send people to hell for not believing in Jesus Christ? Doesn't the Bible say, 'Do not judge, and you will not be judged'? Then why are you being so judgmental?"

They will quote the Bible out of context and twist its meaning. If you want to know the best way to respond to someone who uses deceptive tactics to sidetrack your witness for Christ, read John 4, the story of our Lord's encounter with the Samaritan woman. When Jesus was at Jacob's Well in Samaria, a woman came to draw water. Jesus spoke to her, and she cleverly tried to throw him offtrack. She used the same diversions people use today—but Jesus wasn't taken in by her tactics.

The woman said, in effect, "Jews have no dealings with Samaritans." Jesus let that pass. She said, "Our traditions say thus and so." He ignored it. She said, "The Jews and Samaritans have different belief systems." He refused to get caught up in a debate over whose belief system was right. Jesus was focused on one thing: the woman's desperate spiritual need. She was living a sinful life, and she needed to experience repentance, forgiveness, and a new life of faith. He kept bringing the conversation back to the woman's personal need. He forced her to reexamine her life and to recognize that she had no peace with God. He sidestepped all her clever attempts to change the subject—until at last she surrendered.

Jesus lived in total dependence on the Father. Through prayer, he continually sought the mind of the Father. He continually displayed the wisdom and discernment of the Father, and that is why the woman's deceptive schemes didn't work on him. If Joshua and the elders of Israel had prayed and sought God's counsel, God would have exposed the lies of the Gibeonites. But, verse 14 tells us, Joshua and the elders "did not ask counsel from the LORD."

A teakettle of truth, an ocean of lies

When I gave my life to Jesus Christ in 1964, a friend of mine accepted Christ at the same time. We immediately began to witness to everyone we met. We didn't need to take a course on evangelism. We simply told people what Jesus had done in our lives.

Everyone in the neighborhood knew what a mischievous young man I was before my conversion. All I had to do was tell people how Jesus had changed my life, and people would say, "Wow, really? That's amazing!"

My friend and I started going to the places where we used to hang out. We would talk to our unsaved friends and tell them about the changes Jesus had made in our lives. But as time passed, my friend's passion for sharing Christ waned. He began to slip back into the old worldly patterns. He went back to hanging out with his worldly friends. His behavior changed. His speech changed. He stopped talking to people about Jesus. And within six months, he was fully back in the world.

What happened to this young man? What happened to his intense passion for sharing Jesus Christ with others? Was he laughed at, ridiculed, or persecuted? No, the people that he and I witnessed to were generally polite. They'd listen to us, ask us questions, and talk to us about our beliefs.

And one other thing: *they quoted Scripture.* When we told them something that Jesus had said, they turned right around and countered with another verse from the Bible. Of course, the Scriptures they used were twisted and wrenched out of context. They used the Bible to deceive my friend. So, while he was trying unsuccessfully to win them to Christ, they were winning him back to the world.

Donald Grey Barnhouse told a story from the life of Joseph Duveen, the influential London art dealer of the early twentieth century. Duveen once took his daughter to the beach, but she refused to go into the water because she feared the ocean was too cold. He was sure that, once she went into the water, she'd enjoy it, but he couldn't convince her to try.

So Duveen built a fire on the beach, put a teakettle over the fire, and heated the water in the kettle until it whistled and steamed. He took the steaming teakettle to the water's edge and made sure his daughter watched him as he poured the hot water into the ocean. His plan worked. The little girl went into the water and enjoyed playing in the waves for the rest of the afternoon.

The trick Joseph Duveen played on his little girl may seem harmless, but it illustrates how we are often deceived by the world. False teachers will pour a small amount of comforting truth into an ocean of falsehoods. Then they entice us to go wading in that sea of lies. While we are splashing about in wave after wave of satanic deception, we are being drawn away from our love for God.

As you read the story of Joshua and the Gibeonites, you can't help noticing that Joshua had his suspicions about them. There was a check in his spirit as he listened to their story. When the Gibeonites claimed they had come from a distant city, Joshua had his soldiers look in their bags and examine their wineskins. He doubted their story—but when he examined the evidence, their story seemed to check out. That's because Joshua was looking at the situation from a human perspective.

Even though something bothered him about the Gibeonites' story, Joshua did not go to the Lord and ask for wisdom and discernment. He knew something was not right, but he ignored the alarm bells in the back of his mind.

One of the most dangerous things a Christian can say is, "I can handle this." I have heard Christians say those tragic words again and again, and I cannot think of one time it has turned out for the best. I have heard Christians say, "I can handle this relationship, even though God's Word says it is wrong." I have heard Christians say, "I can handle this temptation." I have heard Christians say, "I can handle this decision without any advice."

Those who take a go-it-alone attitude, who resist all offers of help or Christian counsel, or who resist God's prescription for their problem, inevitably come to grief. They invariably experience remorse and regret. They always seem to say, at some point, "If only I had listened. If only I had asked for help. If only I had asked God for wisdom and discernment. But now it's too late."

A friend once asked me, "What are your strengths?"

"I have none," I said.

"Well, what are your weaknesses?" he said.

"Every area of my life," I said.

That is not false modesty. That is the absolute truth. May God protect me from ever speaking those fateful words, "I can handle it." I know Satan would love nothing more than for me to revel in my "strengths." That is why, like Paul, I choose to revel only in my weaknesses. And that is why you and I must continually pray for discernment to resist the deceitfulness of sin.

Only prayer can open our eyes to the subtle deception of Satan. Only prayer can give us the wisdom to see through the flattering words and manipulative schemes of the ungodly. Only prayer will protect us from that false sense of security we feel during mountaintop experiences. That's why Jesus taught us to pray, "And lead us not into temptation, but deliver us from evil" (Matthew 6:13).

We can't handle this life in our own strength. Our enemy is smarter than we are, and his deceptions are subtle and persuasive. We need to continually ask God to deliver us from the evil one.

Maintain your integrity

Let's take another look at Joshua's response to the Gibeonites after they had deceived him. When the deception was revealed, many of the people wanted to take their revenge against the Gibeonites. Even though Joshua and the leaders of the nation had made a covenant with the Gibeonites, the Israelites reasoned that a covenant based on deception should not be binding. But Joshua and the elders acted with integrity, even though they had been deceived and humiliated.

It could be argued that a contract based on fraud ought to be null and void. Why did the Israelite leaders keep their word, even after they had been defrauded? It's because they did not want to bring disgrace upon God by violating their oath. Joshua punished the Gibeonites for their deception, but he kept his oath to God.

Joshua's actions are instructive and consistent with New Testament teaching. In 1 Corinthians 7, Paul gives the church an injunction about marriage between a believing and unbelieving spouse. He says that if the unbelieving spouse chooses to leave the marriage, then the Christian spouse is not bound to the marriage. But if the unbelieving spouse is willing to remain married, the believer should honor the wedding vows. After all, Paul says, "For how do you know, wife, whether you will save your husband? Or how do you know, husband, whether you will save your wife?" (1 Corinthians 7:16).

A believing spouse might say, "But I wasn't a Christian when I made that vow. I didn't know what I was getting into. I didn't know I would one day accept Christ, and then I would have to go to church alone, pray alone, and raise my children in the faith alone. I didn't know how hard my life would be as a Christian married to an unbeliever."

That's true. But by keeping your wedding vows (even though you made those vows as an unbeliever, not understanding what they would ultimately mean), you are demonstrating a level of faithfulness, integrity, and commitment that bring honor and glory to God. You are keeping a vow you made to him.

(Please understand, there are situations where this general principle might not apply. For example, if your spouse has broken the marriage vow through adultery, or if your spouse is a threat to your safety or the safety of your children, then my counsel to you might be very different.)

You may have taken some wrong turns in your life because you did not ask God for wisdom and discernment. You may have made unwise decisions based on deceptive information. It's impossible to undo the past, but you can start now to make good decisions for the future. If you ask the Lord for wisdom, he will freely give it to you.

So learn from the example of Joshua, including his mistake. When you face a difficult decision, stop and pray: *Lord, what should I do? Please reveal your wisdom to me.* If you sincerely pray that prayer, God will keep you on the path of wisdom.

8

How to Live Victoriously

Joshua 10–12

General Ambrose Burnside was a Union Army general in the Civil War. He led successful military campaigns in North Carolina and Tennessee, and he should have easily won a major victory at Petersburg, Virginia, to dramatically shorten the Civil War. Instead, Burnside engineered one of the worst Union defeats in that war.

By mid-1864, the war had bogged down to a bloody stalemate between North and South. Soldiers were dying by the thousands on both sides, yet neither side could gain the upper hand. So General Burnside suggested a plan for breaking the stalemate at Petersburg. His plan was to tunnel into the Confederate defensive trenches and detonate a large quantity of explosives. This would allow Union troops to enter the trenches and overrun the Confederates. The plan was approved by General Ulysses S. Grant, and Burnside was appointed to implement his plan.

A division of Pennsylvania infantry, which included many experienced coal miners, tunneled beneath Confederate lines. On July

30, 1864, the soldiers detonated a huge cache of explosives. The blast left a 135-foot-wide crater that is still visible today. Nearly three hundred Confederate soldiers died in the blast. The Confederates were caught off guard and a Union victory seemed certain.

Then everything went wrong. A brigade of Union troops under Burnside's subordinate, General James Ledlie, poured through the tunnel and into the crater. Burnside had chosen Ledlie—a proven incompetent—by casting lots. General Ledlie never briefed his troops, so they had no idea what they were to do when they entered the crater. They milled around at the bottom of the hole, waiting for orders that never came. General Ledlie, meanwhile, stayed in his tent, drinking himself into a stupor.

And there were other blunders. General Burnside failed to equip his soldiers with ladders, so when the soldiers emerged from the tunnel, they had no way to get out of the crater. When the Confederates regrouped, they simply gathered around the rim of the crater and fired down at the Union troops—like shooting fish in a barrel. The result: fifty-three hundred Union soldiers were killed or wounded.

What should have been a decisive victory for the North became a symbol of military ineptitude. The disaster ended the careers of Burnside and Ledlie, and the costly siege of Petersburg continued for another eight months. Upon hearing of the disaster at Petersburg, President Lincoln remarked, "Only Burnside could have snatched one more defeat from the jaws of victory."

When I think of General Burnside's failure at Petersburg, I'm reminded that we believers often commit the same mistakes. We have a brilliant strategy, given to us by our Commander-in-Chief, Jesus Christ. We have all the resources we could want, provided by God the Father. We have begun well, and we are poised for victory.

But then our nerve fails, our faith stumbles, and our vision falters. We neglect to claim the complete victory. Like General Burnside, we snatch defeat from the jaws of victory. That's the situation that now confronts Joshua and the people of Israel.

Stopping the sun in its tracks

In these three chapters, Joshua 10 through 12, we find the story of a bloody military campaign. Skeptics often cite this section of the Bible as proof that the God of the Old Testament was a cruel and bloodthirsty deity, in contrast to the New Testament God of love and grace. So I want to answer that criticism and place this section of Joshua in context to show that the God of the Old Testament and the God of the New Testament are one and the same.

If you take an honest look at the pagan Canaanite tribes, you see that they practiced an idolatrous religion that was not only sexually immoral but unimaginably cruel and murderous. In Leviticus, God told Moses, "You shall not do as they do in the land of Egypt, where you lived, and you shall not do as they do in the land of Canaan, to which I am bringing you. You shall not walk in their statutes" (Leviticus 18:3).

In the rest of the chapter, God lists the practices of the Canaanites, which include various forms of incest, bestiality, and sexual perversion. Their practices also included the sin of sacrificing their babies to the god Molech: "You shall not give any of your children to offer them to Molech, and so profane the name of your God: I am the LORD" (Leviticus 18:21).

Molech, also known as Moloch or the sacred bull, was a demonic Canaanite deity represented by an idol made of brass, shaped like a man with a bull's head and outstretched hands. Fires were stoked in the idol's belly or in a brazier beneath the hands. Unbelievable as it may seem, the priests of Molech would place living infants in the fires of the idol.

Archaeologists have confirmed that the Canaanites and Amorites in the region did in fact practice the horrible perversions described in Leviticus. Researchers have also found funerary jars containing the remains of children who were buried alive, their bones bearing mute witness to their awful death agonies as they were suffocated as offerings to the horrific Canaanite deities. The pagan Canaanites had no regard for human life, not even the lives of their own children. So the heart of God was stirred and angered by these practices, and he told the Israelites through Moses:

> "But you shall keep my statutes and my rules and do none of these abominations, either the native or the stranger who sojourns among you (for the people of the land, who were before you, did all of these abominations, so that the land became unclean), lest the land vomit you out when you make it unclean, as it vomited out the nation that was before you. For everyone who does any of these abominations, the persons who do them shall be cut off from among their people. So keep my charge never to practice any of these abominable customs that were practiced before you, and never to make yourselves unclean by them: I am the LORD your God" (Leviticus 18:26-30).

Is it any wonder, then, that God should instruct his people to exterminate these people and their abominable practices? Was God truly bloodthirsty in commanding the destruction of a culture that slaughtered children by fire and suffocation—or was the eradication of those bloodthirsty cultures an act of mercy? God ordered the destruction of those people to prevent Israel from being contaminated by their practices.

The story of the conquest of Canaan began with the destruction of Jericho and Ai. In Joshua 10, we learn of Adoni-zedek, the king of Jerusalem:

As soon as Adoni-zedek, king of Jerusalem, heard how Joshua had captured Ai and had devoted it to destruction, doing to Ai and its king as he had done to Jericho and its king, and how the inhabitants of Gibeon had made peace with Israel and were among them, he feared greatly, because Gibeon was a great city, like one of the royal cities, and because it was greater than Ai, and all its men were warriors. So Adoni-zedek king of Jerusalem sent to Hoham king of Hebron, to Piram king of Jarmuth, to Japhia king of Lachish, and to Debir king of Eglon, saying, "Come up to me and help me, and let us strike Gibeon. For it has made peace with Joshua and with the people of Israel." Then the five kings of the Amorites, the king of Jerusalem, the king of Hebron, the king of Jarmuth, the king of Lachish, and the king of Eglon, gathered their forces and went up with all their armies and encamped against Gibeon and made war against it.

And the men of Gibeon sent to Joshua at the camp in Gilgal, saying, "Do not relax your hand from your servants. Come up to us quickly and save us and help us, for all the kings of the Amorites who dwell in the hill country are gathered against us." So Joshua went up from Gilgal, he and all the people of war with him, and all the mighty men of valor. And the LORD said to Joshua, "Do not fear them, for I have given them into your hands. Not a man of them shall stand before you." So Joshua came upon them suddenly, having marched up all night from Gilgal. And the LORD threw them into a panic before Israel, who struck them with a great blow at Gibeon and chased them by the way of the ascent of Beth-horon and struck them as far as Azekah and Makkedah. And as they fled before Israel, while they were going down the ascent of Beth-horon, the LORD threw down large stones from heaven on them as far as Azekah, and they died. There were more who died because of the hailstones than the sons of Israel killed with the sword.

At that time Joshua spoke to the LORD in the day when the LORD gave the Amorites over to the sons of Israel, and he said in the sight of Israel,

"Sun, stand still at Gibeon,
and moon, in the Valley of Aijalon."
And the sun stood still, and the moon stopped,
until the nation took vengeance on their enemies.

Is this not written in the Book of Jashar? The sun stopped in the midst of heaven and did not hurry to set for about a whole day. There has been no day like it before or since, when the LORD heeded the voice of a man, for the LORD fought for Israel.

So Joshua returned, and all Israel with him, to the camp at Gilgal (10:1-15).

Adoni-zedek, the king of Jerusalem, formed an alliance with four other Amorite kings, and together they made war against Gibeon. So the Gibeonites sent a message to Joshua, pleading for help. Joshua marched his army through the night to Gibeon. Along the way, the Lord told Joshua not to be afraid of the Amorites because he would deliver the enemy into Joshua's hands. Joshua arrived in Gibeon, taking the Amorites by surprise, and attacking with deadly ferocity. The Lord threw the Amorites into confusion, and the Israelites pursued them along the roads. Then the Lord also sent hailstones down upon the Amorites, and more of them died from the hailstorm than from the Israelites' swords.

As the battle raged, Joshua called upon the Lord, praying that the sun would stand still in the sky. So time itself seemed to stop while Israel destroyed the Amorites. The wording in verse 13 (which states that the sun "stopped in the midst of heaven...for about a whole day") suggests that the sun was directly overhead—high noon—when it stopped.

This passage describes the greatest miracle since the creation of the world. Today, of course, we know that the appearance of the sun moving across the sky is actually the result of the earth rotating on its axis. So in order for the sun to appear to stand still in the sky, it would seem that the earth would have had to stop rotating on its axis for the length of a day, then resume its rotation once more. There is no question that such a miraculous event would involve an extreme intervention in the laws of physics.

For example, this miracle would require the suspension of the principle of conservation of angular momentum. The earth rotates because it has a great deal of rotational kinetic energy (angular momentum). If you suddenly stop the earth's rotation, all of that energy has to go someplace—with catastrophic results. The oceans would be hurled out of their sea beds, sending vast mega-tsunamis rolling eastward across the continents. The atmosphere would be converted into a global hurricane with winds of roughly a thousand miles an hour. The solid ground beneath our feet would turn gelatinous as the earth's crust liquefied. All living things and all the works of man would be destroyed in an instant—unless God intervened in the laws of physics to preserve life on earth.

And that's exactly what God did. It's important to note that several ancient cultures have myths that apparently are intended to account for Joshua's long day. A Greek myth, recorded by the Roman poet Ovid in his *Metamorphoses* (Book II), tells how Phaëton, the son of the sun god Helios, drove the shining chariot of the sun around the sky for a full day. The lingering of the sun-chariot in the sky caused disasters across the Earth until Zeus felled Phaëton with a thunderbolt.

On the other side of the world, the Chinese recorded an event during the reign of Yao (at roughly the same time that Joshua lived) in which the sun stood in place above the horizon for so long that Chinese astronomers believed it might set the world on fire. And the Maori indigenous people of New Zealand have a myth of Maui, an ancient hero who snared the sun and held it captive for a long time before he finally allowed it to rise in the morning sky.

It's significant that the Amorites, like most of the Canaanite tribes, worshipped the sun and the moon. In this account, we read that Joshua commanded, "Sun, stand still at Gibeon, and moon, in the Valley of Aijalon." To my mind, this miracle rings true because the very deities the Amorites worshipped were forced to obey Joshua's God, the God of Israel. Joshua's long day is not just a magic trick meant to frighten and impress the Canaanites. This miracle has a significant point to make. It's a meaningful demonstration of God's superiority and authority over the false gods of the Canaanites.

You have probably heard the urban legend that NASA computers have confirmed that there is a missing day in the celestial calendar, corresponding to the long day of Joshua. This urban legend has found its way into my email inbox many times. Please do not repeat this story as "proof" that the Bible is true, because the story itself is false. The rocket scientists at NASA are very smart people with highly advanced computers, but there is no way that *any* computer could determine that a day is missing from the calendar of the universe.

The truth of God's Word does not need to be "confirmed" by lies. We have already seen instances where genuine archaeological discoveries have confirmed the historical reliability of the Bible. I can't explain how God performed the miracle of Joshua's long day any more than I can explain how Jesus turned water into wine. The very inexplicable nature of these events is what makes them miracles. If we could explain them, they wouldn't be miracles.

If anyone asks you to explain how God stopped the sun in the sky in Joshua 10, don't feel you have to offer a scientific explanation. There is no scientific explanation. All we can say is that God's Word tells us that Joshua prayed and God intervened. What we do understand about God's Word is convincing enough that we can trust God for the things we cannot understand.

The battle is the Lord's

Next, we learn the fate of the five Amorite kings:

> These five kings fled and hid themselves in the cave at Makkedah. And it was told to Joshua, "The five kings have been found, hidden in the cave at Makkedah." And Joshua said, "Roll large stones against the mouth of the cave and set men by it to guard them, but do not stay there yourselves. Pursue your enemies; attack their rear guard. Do not let them enter their cities, for the LORD your God has given them into your hand." When Joshua and the sons of Israel had finished striking them with a great blow until they were wiped out, and when the remnant that remained of them had entered into the fortified cities, then all the people returned safe to Joshua in the camp at Makkedah. Not a man moved his tongue against any of the people of Israel.
>
> Then Joshua said, "Open the mouth of the cave and bring those five kings out to me from the cave." And they did so, and brought those five kings out to him from the cave, the king of Jerusalem, the king of Hebron, the king of Jarmuth, the king of Lachish, and the king of Eglon. And when they brought those kings out to Joshua, Joshua summoned all the men of Israel and said to the chiefs of the men of war who had gone with him, "Come near; put your feet on the necks of these kings." Then they came near and put their feet on their necks. And Joshua said to

them, "Do not be afraid or dismayed; be strong and courageous. For thus the LORD will do to all your enemies
against whom you fight." And afterward Joshua struck
them and put them to death, and he hanged them on
five trees. And they hung on the trees until evening. But
at the time of the going down of the sun, Joshua commanded, and they took them down from the trees and
threw them into the cave where they had hidden themselves, and they set large stones against the mouth of the
cave, which remain to this very day.

As for Makkedah, Joshua captured it on that day and
struck it, and its king, with the edge of the sword. He
devoted to destruction every person in it; he left none
remaining. And he did to the king of Makkedah just as he
had done to the king of Jericho (10:16-28).

Once the battle is over and the enemy forces have been completely destroyed, Joshua turns his attention to the five Amorite
kings who started the war. Here, we see some of the ancient Middle Eastern customs that were practiced by the victors over the vanquished. Joshua had the defeated kings prostrate themselves in the
dust, and then he called his commanders to place their feet on the
necks of the defeated kings—a symbol of total victory over the foe.
Then Joshua said to his people (echoing the words of encouragement God had spoken to Joshua), "Do not be afraid or dismayed;
be strong and courageous. For thus the LORD will do to all your enemies against whom you fight."

Then Joshua ordered the five kings executed by hanging. With
the execution of the five kings of the "axis of evil," Israel's victory
over the Amorites was complete. But there were still other enemies
to be fought in southern Canaan:

Then Joshua and all Israel with him passed on from
Makkedah to Libnah and fought against Libnah. And the

LORD gave it also and its king into the hand of Israel. And he struck it with the edge of the sword, and every person in it; he left none remaining in it. And he did to its king as he had done to the king of Jericho.

Then Joshua and all Israel with him passed on from Libnah to Lachish and laid siege to it and fought against it. And the LORD gave Lachish into the hand of Israel, and he captured it on the second day and struck it with the edge of the sword, and every person in it, as he had done to Libnah.

Then Horam king of Gezer came up to help Lachish. And Joshua struck him and his people, until he left none remaining.

Then Joshua and all Israel with him passed on from Lachish to Eglon. And they laid siege to it and fought against it. And they captured it on that day, and struck it with the edge of the sword. And he devoted every person in it to destruction that day, as he had done to Lachish.

Then Joshua and all Israel with him went up from Eglon to Hebron. And they fought against it and captured it and struck it with the edge of the sword, and its king and its towns, and every person in it. He left none remaining, as he had done to Eglon, and devoted it to destruction and every person in it.

Then Joshua and all Israel with him turned back to Debir and fought against it and he captured it with its king and all its towns. And they struck them with the edge of the sword and devoted to destruction every person in it; he left none remaining. Just as he had done to Hebron and to Libnah and its king, so he did to Debir and to its king.

So Joshua struck the whole land, the hill country and the Negeb and the lowland and the slopes, and all their kings. He left none remaining, but devoted to destruction all that breathed, just as the LORD God of Israel commanded. And Joshua struck them from Kadesh-barnea as far as Gaza, and all the country of Goshen, as far as Gibeon. And Joshua captured all these kings and their land at one time, because the LORD God of Israel fought for Israel. Then Joshua returned, and all Israel with him, to the camp at Gilgal (10:29-43).

By the end of Joshua 10, the nation of Israel occupies all of southern Canaan, from the hill country to the southern desert (the Negeb or Negev), from the western foothills to the mountain slopes. How did Israel conquer these territories? Verse 42 tells us: "And Joshua captured all these kings and their land at one time, because the LORD God of Israel fought for Israel." This is a theme that threads its way throughout Scripture: The battle is the Lord's. He fights for his people. Our part is to simply obey him and possess the land. If we rely on his strength, not ours, he will fight for us—and we cannot lose.

Rest from war

In Joshua 11, after Israel has conquered the southern region of Canaan, Jabin, king of Hazor, forms an alliance with the kings of the north. Once again, Joshua must lead his people into battle:

When Jabin, king of Hazor, heard of this, he sent to Jobab king of Madon, and to the king of Shimron, and to the king of Achshaph, and to the kings who were in the northern hill country, and in the Arabah south of Chinneroth, and in the lowland, and in Naphoth-dor on the west, to the Canaanites in the east and the west, the Amorites, the Hittites, the Perizzites, and the Jebusites in the hill country, and the Hivites under Hermon in the land of Mizpah. And they came out with all their troops, a great horde, in number like the sand that is on the seashore, with very many horses and chariots. And all these kings joined their forces and came and encamped together at the waters of Merom to fight against Israel.

And the L ORD said to Joshua, "Do not be afraid of them, for tomorrow at this time I will give over all of them, slain, to Israel. You shall hamstring their horses and burn their chariots with fire." So Joshua and all his warriors came suddenly against them by the waters of Merom and fell upon them. And the L ORD gave them into the hand of Israel, who struck them and chased them as far as Great Sidon and Misrephoth-maim, and eastward as far as the Valley of Mizpeh. And they struck them until he left none remaining. And Joshua did to them just as the L ORD said to him: he hamstrung their horses and burned their chariots with fire.

And Joshua turned back at that time and captured Hazor and struck its king with the sword, for Hazor formerly was the head of all those kingdoms. And they struck with the sword all who were in it, devoting them to destruction; there was none left that breathed. And he burned Hazor with fire. And all the cities of those kings, and all their kings, Joshua captured, and struck them with the edge of the sword, devoting them to destruction, just as Moses the servant of the L ORD had commanded. But none of the cities that stood on mounds did Israel burn, except Hazor alone; that Joshua burned. And all the spoil of these cities and the livestock, the people of Israel took for their plunder. But every person they struck with the edge of the sword until they had destroyed them, and they did not leave any who breathed. Just as the L ORD had commanded Moses his servant, so Moses commanded Joshua, and so Joshua did. He left nothing undone of all that the L ORD had commanded Moses.

So Joshua took all that land, the hill country and all the Negeb and all the land of Goshen and the lowland and the Arabah and the hill country of Israel and its lowland from Mount Halak, which rises toward Seir, as far as Baal-gad in the Valley of Lebanon below Mount Hermon. And he captured all their kings and struck them and put them to death. Joshua made war a long time with all those kings. There was not a city that made peace with the people of Israel except the Hivites, the inhabitants of Gibeon. They took them all in battle. For it was the LORD's doing to harden their hearts that they should come against Israel in battle, in order that they should be devoted to destruction and should receive no mercy but be destroyed, just as the LORD commanded Moses.

And Joshua came at that time and cut off the Anakim from the hill country, from Hebron, from Debir, from Anab, and from all the hill country of Judah, and from all the hill country of Israel. Joshua devoted them to destruction with their cities. There was none of the Anakim left in the land of the people of Israel. Only in Gaza, in Gath, and in Ashdod did some remain. So Joshua took the whole land, according to all that the LORD had spoken to Moses. And Joshua gave it for an inheritance to Israel according to their tribal allotments. And the land had rest from war (11:1-23).

Once again, in verse 6, we see the repeated refrain of the book of Joshua: "And the LORD said to Joshua, 'Do not be afraid of them.'"

This theme in Joshua reminds me of King Christian X of Denmark, who reigned from 1912 through 1947. During World War II, when the Nazis occupied Denmark, he was imprisoned by the Germans for refusing to accommodate the Nazi oppression of the Jews. One day, shortly before he was imprisoned, King Christian saw a Nazi flag over a government building in Copenhagen. He called the German commandant and demanded the flag be removed. The commandant refused. "Then a Danish solder will take the flag down," the king replied. The commandant replied, "We will shoot him." The king replied, "I think not, for I shall be that soldier." The commandant had the flag taken down.

Whether God is speaking to Joshua, or to King Christian, or to everyday Christians like you and me, his message is the same: "Do not be afraid of them. Be courageous and obedient to God's calling."

Joshua was courageous and obedient. He and his army obeyed God and surprised the enemy at the waters of Merom. Again, the victorious army of Israel pursued the enemy along the roads and down the valleys and over the hills, leaving no survivors. The Scriptures sum up the battle in these words:

> Just as the LORD had commanded Moses his servant, so Moses commanded Joshua, and so Joshua did. He left nothing undone of all that the LORD had commanded Moses…So Joshua took the whole land, according to all that the LORD had spoken to Moses. And Joshua gave it for an inheritance to Israel according to their tribal allotments. And the land had rest from war (11:15,23).

What a beautiful, refreshing statement: "And the land had rest from war." After a time of intense conflict and struggle, there came a time of rest and peace. If you are going through a struggle right now, if you feel your faith is being stretched, your obedience is being tested, and you wonder when these trials will end, you have this assurance: A day will come when you, like Joshua and the Israelites, will have rest from war. A time of refreshment is coming.

Our defeated foe

Joshua 12 lists the kings and peoples defeated under the leadership of both Moses and Joshua—and it's a lengthy list. Rather than reproduce it here, I suggest you take a look at that chapter in your own Bible.

You may wonder, *What does this long list of bloody conquests have to do with my life as a follower of Jesus Christ in the twenty-first century?*

That question is easily answered. There's a single theme that runs through these three chapters in Joshua—the theme of *victory*.

In Joshua's day, battles were fought with swords and shields. Victory meant that wicked kings were vanquished and wicked cities were conquered. But God has a very different form of victory in mind for you and me. Victory, in the New Testament sense, does not involve a battle against flesh and blood. Our fight is waged against spiritual powers and forces.

We sometimes think we are at war against human enemies, human institutions, and human political systems. Some people want to take God's name out of the Pledge of Allegiance or ban after-school Bible clubs, and we think those people are the enemy. While it's important to defend our religious freedom, we should never view any human as our enemy. We must never forget that "we do not wrestle against flesh and blood, but against the rulers, against the authorities, against the cosmic powers over this present darkness, against the spiritual forces of evil in the heavenly places" (Ephesians 6:12).

Our enemy is Satan and his rebellious angels. We are at war against spiritual strongholds of evil. And we easily forget that the victory has already been won. Satan is a defeated foe. He has been vanquished by Jesus Christ. Even so, he's still dangerous. Satan causes conflicts among believers, stirs up hostility against us, and tempts us and tries to distract us from our mission. Satan knows he has little time left before he is consigned to the fires of eternal punishment.

Now we must ask ourselves: Have we claimed the complete victory that is already ours in Jesus Christ? Have we claimed the complete victory so we can finish this mopping-up operation against our defeated foe? Have we claimed the complete victory so we can experience victorious living in the here and now?

This is no time for a defeatist attitude. This is no time to let up. We must not surrender to discouragement or pessimism. Our enemy is on the run. There's no escape for him. We have him where we want him. Like Joshua, let's take the entire land that God has promised as our inheritance. Once we possess the land, we will finally have rest from our long spiritual war.

How to claim victory

What do I mean when I say we must take the land God has promised us? How do we claim the victory? We do so by relentlessly, obediently pursuing our mission for Jesus Christ. We don't retreat. We don't give in to temptation and sinful habits. We refuse to be intimidated when we witness for Christ. We never forget that we are engaged in a spiritual struggle against spiritual strongholds. This is war, and we must conduct ourselves as soldiers, but with the confidence that our general has already won.

The church of Jesus Christ was never meant to be a USO show to entertain the troops. It was never meant to be a weekend pass so the soldiers can enjoy some R and R. The church is the headquarters for an all-out offensive against Satan. We are on the spiritual battlefront, engaged in a great struggle for the souls of men, women, and young people. Our mission is to rescue the perishing, heal the wounded, and liberate the prisoners. Our objective is to break the chains of sin and addiction, and to lead the way to victory, liberation, and a life of meaning and joy.

Yes, the victory has already been won on the cross at Calvary, but we must claim the complete victory for our own lives and the lives of those around us. God the Son emptied himself of the glory he had in heaven. He was born of a virgin, lived for thirty-three years on earth, carried out his mission in Palestine, was crucified on a criminal's cross, was buried in a borrowed tomb, rose again on the third day, and ascended into heaven. Soon he is coming back. He did not go through all of this so that we would live defeated lives.

From Genesis to Revelation, God's message to us is that he has made it possible for us to experience complete victory, both in this life and the life to come. He has not given us a partial victory or an occasional victory but *total* victory. It's up to us to claim the victory for our lives, day by day.

There is a story told about a company of soldiers in the Korean War. Whether the story is true, I can't say, but it illustrates an important point. Baker Company was cut off from other American units and was surrounded by enemy forces. The American military headquarters received no word from Baker Company for several hours. The radio corpsman at headquarters kept calling, "Baker Company, do you read? Baker Company, do you read?"

Finally, a faint reply came through the static. "This is Baker Company."

"What is your situation?" the corpsman asked.

"The enemy is to the east of us…and to the north of us…and to the west of us…and to the south of us…They can't get away from us now!"

Sometimes, we feel hemmed in on all sides by the enemy of our souls. At such times, we need to remember that we face a defeated foe. He may have us surrounded, but all that means is that he can't get away from us now. All we have to do is claim the victory that has already been won.

Is it time to panic? Is it time for despair? Is it time to surrender? Or is victory within our grasp? Remember the words of the apostle Paul:

> We are afflicted in every way, but not crushed; perplexed, but not driven to despair; persecuted, but not forsaken; struck down, but not destroyed…
>
> So we do not lose heart. Though our outer self is wasting away, our inner self is being renewed day by day.

For this light momentary affliction is preparing for us an eternal weight of glory beyond all comparison, as we look not to the things that are seen but to the things that are unseen. For the things that are seen are transient, but the things that are unseen are eternal (2 Corinthians 4:8-9,16-18).

Like Paul, we are hard pressed on every side, but we know the victory has been won. The opposition we face is temporary, but our victory is eternal. We are surrounded by opposition, by antagonists who hate God's truth—but they can't get away from us now. Our mission is not to destroy them but to win them to Christ. We won't retreat, because we are already conquerors. We have nothing to fear and everything to celebrate.

In Joshua 10–12, we find three important principles for the spiritual battles we face:

- Principle 1: War begins with confrontation.
- Principle 2: War is conflict.
- Principle 3: War concludes with conquest.

Let's apply these principles to our daily spiritual battles.

Principle 1: War begins with confrontation. Joshua and the army of Israel were surrounded by a united enemy. Tribes and kings who normally fought among themselves banded together against Israel. The various Canaanite tribes set aside their differences to attack the people of God. Joshua knew God had promised victory to Israel, but first there had to be confrontation.

The historian Josephus estimates that the Israelites faced three hundred thousand foot soldiers, ten thousand cavalry, and twenty thousand chariots. For the nation of Israel, the Promised Land was hostile territory. From a human perspective, the odds were stacked against them. Any military strategist would have told Joshua his situation was hopeless. But God told Joshua the victory was already won—and Joshua trusted God's promise.

This same principle applies to all our battles. You may feel paralyzed by a confrontation in your life. If so, you are looking at this challenge from a purely human perspective. You have left Jehovah out of the equation. Don't ever go to war without taking God with you.

Principle 2: War is conflict. Don't be afraid of conflict. Take the battle to your enemy. Wage war against Satan, confident that the Lord goes before you into battle.

Joshua didn't wait for the battle to come to him. He took the battle to the enemy. Yes, his people faced thousands of soldiers, cavalry, and chariots—and Joshua was no super-saint. He was a human being, subject to all the same fears and doubts that you and I experience. That's why there are two moments in these three chapters where God encourages Joshua. In Joshua 10:25, God says, "Do not be afraid or dismayed; be strong and courageous." And in Joshua 11:6, God says, "Do not be afraid of them."

God knows how our minds work. He understood the turmoil in Joshua's heart. So two times in this section God said to Joshua, "Do not be afraid," and he followed each assurance with a promise of victory. Here's an important principle of Scripture study: The Lord never wastes his words. He does not tell people, "Do not be afraid," unless the people are afraid. Whenever God or one of his angels says, "Do not be afraid," you can be sure that someone's knees are knocking.

When the Lord appeared to Abram (later called Abraham) to make a covenant with him, his opening words were, "Fear not" (Genesis 15:1). When the Lord appeared to Abraham's son, Isaac, he said again, "Fear not" (Genesis 26:24). When Jacob was afraid to go down to Egypt, God said, "Do not be afraid" (Genesis 46:3). When Moses faced war with the Amorites, God said, "Do not fear him" (Numbers 21:34). When God sent Elijah to confront an idolatrous king, he said, "Do not be afraid of him" (2 Kings 1:15).

When the angel appeared to Mary, the mother of Jesus, the angel said, "Do not be afraid" (Luke 1:30). When the angel appeared to shepherds in the fields and announced the birth of the Savior, he said, "Fear not" (Luke 2:10). God told Paul, when he faced opposition in Corinth, "Do not be afraid, but go on speaking and do not be silent" (Acts 18:9). When Paul was a prisoner aboard a ship that was floundering in a raging storm, God sent an angel to him with the message, "Do not be afraid" (Acts 27:24).

We tend to think that the heroes of the Bible are super-saints who never knew the meaning of fear. That's simply not true. Our Old and New Testament heroes had shaky hands, fluttering stomachs, and stammering tongues, just as we do. So the next time you feel afraid, remember you're in good company. The great heroes of the Bible are trembling and stammering right along with you!

But also remember that the Lord himself is at your side. He says, "Don't be afraid. The victory is already yours." So claim the victory. Stay on the offensive for Christ. Take the battle to the enemy. Advance the kingdom of Christ and rescue lost souls from the enemy's grip. Do this—and you will have victory in all areas of your life. Your prayer life will be vibrant. Your worship will be meaningful. Your fellowship will be dynamic. And every day of your walk with Christ will be an exciting new adventure.

Principle 3: War concludes with conquest. When the conquest has been achieved, when the victory has been won, we can finally have rest from war.

I'm reminded of a story from the early history of colonial Australia. The first Australian-born explorer was Hamilton Hume (1797–1873). In late 1824, Hume led an expedition to map the region known as New South Wales. His goal was to move southeast through the interior until the expedition reached the southern coast of Australia.

Along the way, Hume and his men came face-to-face with a mountain range that blocked their way. Exhausted and discouraged, Hume's men begged him to give up and turn back. Hume pointed to the high mountain ahead and said, "If we attain that summit, I know we'll see the ocean. We'll find what we are looking for, and we can return home and tell others of our success."

So Hume and his men climbed the mountain. Reaching the summit, they looked out—but there was no ocean. They saw nothing but miles and miles of ridges and forests. They marked the location of the mountain on their map and named it Mount Disappointment. Then they continued moving on.

The Hume expedition eventually reached Corio Bay. They reported that the interior of Australia was habitable. Soon, settlers streamed into the outback. The formidable mountain range that made Hume's men want to turn back is known as the Hume Range, and millions now drive the Hume Highway from Sydney to Melbourne.

Life is filled with Mount Disappointments. You have the choice to climb your mountains of disappointment by God's power—or to give up. Whatever your Mount Disappointment may be, God calls you to conquer it. He wants us to trust in him and possess the land he has promised us.

When Satan confronts you, don't be afraid. Stand your ground. The enemy is already defeated. Take the battle to your foe, and God will give you the complete victory.

9

The Cosmic Real Estate Developer

Joshua 13–14

In 1993, I was invited to a breakfast hosted by the Atlanta chapter of the Urban Land Institute, an organization of real estate professionals. They asked me to give a brief talk and then lead in prayer. As I looked out over the crowd, the expressions I saw seemed to say, "Who is this guy?"

So I began by saying, "My name is Michael Youssef, and I work for the largest real estate developer in the universe. I talk to him every day about helping you guys with your real estate deals, and I ask him to give you a part of his action." After I said those words, you could have heard a pin drop. Then I led in prayer.

Most of the people got my point. They knew I was talking about the Heavenly Real Estate Developer, and that I wanted each person in that room to become a partner with God and a stakeholder in his kingdom. But a few people missed the point. They came to me later, handed me their business cards, and said, "If we can do business with your boss, please have him call me at this number." Since I was from the Middle East, they assumed I had connections with an Arab trillionaire!

I wasn't trying to fool anybody. My Boss really is the largest real estate developer in the universe. He gives each of us a territory to operate in. As we come to the next section of Joshua, we see that chapters 13 through 17 are all about real estate. God wants us to put our trust in him, because he is the Cosmic Real Estate Developer.

By God's might, the people of Israel have crossed over the river of impossibility. They have shouted down the walls of Jericho. They have cleansed the land of the polluted practices of the Canaanite religions. They have claimed complete victory. Now one thing remains undone: they must divide the Land of Promise among the tribes of Israel.

This is the land God had promised to Abraham four centuries earlier. He had commanded them not only to conquer the land, but to distribute the land among the people. Joshua 13 through 17 explains how the land was to be divided. We won't dwell on the details or reproduce the full biblical text here, though I suggest you take a look at this section in your own Bible. But we can draw some vital lessons from this passage.

God is not arbitrary

As Joshua 13 opens, we see that much time has passed since the end of the previous chapter. Joshua is an old man, and the Lord speaks to him about apportioning the land:

> Now Joshua was old and advanced in years, and the LORD said to him, "You are old and advanced in years, and there remains yet very much land to possess" (13:1)

The Lord then describes the land that remains for Israel to take over and concludes with these words of promise and instruction:

> "I myself will drive them out from before the people of Israel. Only allot the land to Israel for an inheritance, as I have commanded you. Now therefore divide this land for an inheritance to the nine tribes and half the tribe of Manasseh" (13:6-7).

Joshua divided the Promised Land among the tribes of Israel as God instructed (see 13:8-33), and every tribe except the Levites received a tract of real estate (13:33). And here we find a vital lesson for our lives: God gives us our territory—our blessings and opportunities—according to our measure of faith. The Scriptures tell us, "Every good gift and every perfect gift is from above, coming down from the Father of lights with whom there is no variation or shadow due to change" (James 1:17). And Paul writes,

> Therefore it says,
> "When [Jesus] ascended on high he led a host of captives,
>   and he gave gifts to men."
>
> (Ephesians 4:8)

God wants his children to discover their gifts, use their gifts, invest their gifts, and put their gifts to work for his kingdom.

You may ask, "How does God divide territories among his children today? How do I know what my territory is? How does God divide opportunities and blessings among his people today?" Answer: God does not divide up his territories arbitrarily. He distributes them on the basis of each believer's faithfulness to him.

We see this principle in the example of the tribe of Reuben. According to ancient Hebrew custom, the firstborn is entitled to a double portion of the inheritance. But the tribe of Reuben, the firstborn of Israel, received a smaller and less desirable portion of the land (13:15-23). Why? Reuben, the ancestor of the Reubenite tribe, had sinned against his father, Jacob, committing sexual sin with Bilhah, the servant of Jacob's wife Rachel (see Genesis 35:22). Years later, as Jacob lay dying, he told his eldest son:

> "Reuben, you are my firstborn,
>   my might, and the firstfruits of my strength,
>   preeminent in dignity and preeminent in power.
> Unstable as water, you shall not have preeminence,
>   because you went up to your father's bed;
>   then you defiled it—he went up to my couch!"
>   (Genesis 49:3-4)

According to Hebrew tradition, an extra portion of an inheritance should be given to the eldest simply because of birth order. But God is not bound by human tradition. He looks upon the heart. He judges our works. So the tribe of Reuben received a smaller portion because of Reuben's unfaithfulness. God allocated Reuben's territory in this way to illustrate a spiritual principle: our faithfulness (or unfaithfulness) determines the territory we receive. The sincerity of our hearts determines the level of responsibility and blessing God gives us.

The Levites—the tribe of Levi—received no land whatsoever. This is not a punishment but an honor for the priests who are called by God to minister to all of Israel, regardless of tribal boundaries. The Scriptures explain, "But to the tribe of Levi Moses gave no inheritance; the LORD God of Israel is their inheritance, just as he said to them" (Joshua 13:33). The estate given to the Levites was a spiritual estate, not real estate.

In Joshua 21, we will see the Levites receive an inheritance of forty-two cities, which are distributed among the other tribes throughout the length and breadth of the Promised Land. (This includes the cities of refuge, which we will discuss in chapter 11.) The Levites received these cities instead of territories because they were to serve as the priests and spiritual teachers of the Israelites. The other tribes would farm the land, and the Levites would live on the tithes and offerings the other tribes would bring.

As you look at the inheritance apportioned to the Reubenites and the Levites, does it seem that God is unfair? After all, God gave the Reubenites a smaller portion because their ancestor sinned long before they were born. Why should they be penalized for the sin of Reuben? And what about the Levites? It sounds nice that God is their inheritance—but how would you feel if everyone else got vineyards, orchards, and a hilltop castle, and Joshua said, "You don't get any property because God is your estate"? Would you think it was fair?

You might say, as some skeptics claim, "God's actions seem arbitrary and unjust. Doesn't God understand that a lopsided distribution of land will cause only bitterness and envy among his people?" But God is not unjust. His ways are not our ways because his wisdom is deeper than ours. God sees the past, present, and future as one; we don't. He knows the secrets of every human heart; we don't.

Our understanding is partial, imperfect, and subjective. God's viewpoint is omniscient, flawless, and objective. Even when his decisions make little or no sense to us, we can trust his judgment to be perfect every time.

Three money managers

God blessed each of the tribes of Israel with an inheritance, and he expected each tribe to possess that inheritance and use it to serve him, to establish their families, and to bless future generations. There's a New Testament parallel to the distribution of inheritances in a parable the Lord Jesus told in Matthew 25:14-30, the story of the boss and the three money managers.

In the Lord's parable, a wealthy boss entrusts a substantial amount of money to three employees, three money managers. To put it in today's terms, the boss gave one of them somewhere around $2.5 million, another $1 million, and another $500,000. Was this boss unfair? No. He knew the character and capabilities of each employee.

The man who was entrusted with $2.5 million invested his money and brought back a return of $2.5 million more—he doubled the investment. And the man entrusted with $1 million invested his money and brought back a return of $1 million more—he also doubled his investment. The boss commended each of these money managers with the same words: "Well done, good and faithful servant. You have been faithful over a little; I will set you over much. Enter into the joy of your master."

And the employee who had received only $500,000? When he received the smallest quantity of money, even though it was still a sizable sum, he held a pity party. Those words aren't in the Bible, but I believe that's exactly what this man did. He said to himself, "Poor me! The boss didn't give me as much as he gave those other guys. What am I supposed to do with this chicken feed? The boss doesn't trust me. This is unfair!"

So this employee took his $500,000, dug a hole in the backyard, and buried it. He didn't invest it. He didn't double it. He didn't do anything with it. He foolishly put it in a hole in the ground and covered it with dirt. Would the third money manager have done any differently had he been given $1 million or $2.5 million? Unlikely. The boss had given him the smallest quantity of money because he knew that the third money manager could not be trusted with a larger sum.

So it is with you and me. If we are not faithful with the small things, how can we be trusted with the big things? But the good servant, who is faithful in a few things, will be placed in charge of many things. As Jesus said, the good servant will share in the joy of his Master and Lord, both in this life and in the life to come.

When God gives you a small blessing, a small opportunity to minister, a small territory in which to work, he is watching to see how you handle it. All of your future blessings and opportunities depend on how you handle the challenges he gives you today.

The example of Caleb

In Joshua 14, we find that Joshua's longtime comrade, Caleb, was singled out for a special gift—the greatest and most desirable territory.

> These are the inheritances that the people of Israel received in the land of Canaan, which Eleazar the priest and Joshua the son of Nun and the heads of the fathers' houses of the tribes of the people of Israel gave them to inherit. Their inheritance was by lot, just as the LORD had commanded by the hand of Moses for the nine and one-half tribes. For Moses had given an inheritance to the two and one-half tribes beyond the Jordan, but to the Levites he gave no inheritance among them. For the people of Joseph were two tribes, Manasseh and Ephraim. And no portion was given to the Levites in the land, but only cities to dwell in, with their pasturelands for their livestock and their substance. The people of Israel did as the LORD commanded Moses; they allotted the land.
>
> Then the people of Judah came to Joshua at Gilgal. And Caleb the son of Jephunneh the Kenizzite said to him, "You know what the LORD said to Moses the man of God in Kadesh-barnea concerning you and me. I was

forty years old when Moses the servant of the LORD sent me from Kadesh-barnea to spy out the land, and I brought him word again as it was in my heart. But my brothers who went up with me made the heart of the people melt; yet I wholly followed the LORD my God. And Moses swore on that day, saying, 'Surely the land on which your foot has trodden shall be an inheritance for you and your children forever, because you have wholly followed the LORD my God.' And now, behold, the LORD has kept me alive, just as he said, these forty-five years since the time that the LORD spoke this word to Moses, while Israel walked in the wilderness. And now, behold, I am this day eighty-five years old. I am still as strong today as I was in the day that Moses sent me; my strength now is as my strength was then, for war and for going and coming. So now give me this hill country of which the LORD spoke on that day, for you heard on that day how the Anakim were there, with great fortified cities. It may be that the LORD will be with me, and I shall drive them out just as the LORD said."

Then Joshua blessed him, and he gave Hebron to Caleb the son of Jephunneh for an inheritance. Therefore Hebron became the inheritance of Caleb the son of Jephunneh the Kenizzite to this day, because he wholly followed the LORD, the God of Israel. Now the name of Hebron formerly was Kiriath-arba. (Arba was the greatest man among the Anakim.) And the land had rest from war (14:1-15).

Caleb is a role model and a challenge to us all. We should ask ourselves, "Why was Caleb singled out by God? Why did he receive a larger portion than the rest? What can we learn from the example of Caleb?" We need to understand who Caleb was and what he did.

When the Israelites were in the wilderness, Moses sent out a team of twelve spies to explore the Promised Land (Numbers 13).

Moses approached this mission in a democratic fashion, asking each of the twelve tribes to select one representative. The twelve men went in and examined the agricultural and economic possibilities of the land. They looked at the cities and defenses of the Canaanites. Then they returned and presented two separate reports—a majority report and a minority report.

When the vote was taken among them, the vote was ten to two. Ten of the twelve spies said, in effect, "The land is full of giants. Those guys are huge! They'll eat our lunch! We're no match for them. We would have been better off if we had died in the wilderness." The majority report was nothing but doom and gloom.

But the remaining two spies argued, "So what if the Canaanites all look like body builders and fight like Navy SEALs? They're no more than gnats compared to God! The Lord has promised to go with us—and if God leads us, no enemy can stand against us!"

The minority was right—but the majority prevailed. You probably know who those two courageous and faithful spies were: Joshua and Caleb. These two men were later singled out for great faithfulness to God. Joshua became the successor to Moses during the conquest of the Promised Land, and Caleb was singled out for honor when the real estate was distributed.

A man of optimistic faith

God loves to see us stretch our faith. He loves optimistic believers who trust in him. He loves to see us stepping out, daring great things for him, trusting in his promises. We make God happy when we live by a childlike trust in him.

Caleb was a man of optimistic faith. Where ten other men saw giants, Caleb saw gnats. Where ten other men saw obstacles, Caleb saw opportunities. Where ten other men saw terror, Caleb saw power. Where ten other men saw impossibility, Caleb saw the promise of God. Where ten other men saw defeat, Caleb saw certain victory. Where ten other men saw a bleak future, Caleb saw the God who holds the future. Where ten other men saw hopelessness, Caleb beheld the God of hope.

In Joshua 14, Caleb goes to Joshua and says, in effect, "I was forty years old when Moses sent us out to spy out the land. You and I brought back an optimistic report, but the other ten spies were such pessimists that their report melted the courage of our people. I have always followed God with all my heart. That's why Moses promised that the land I walk on would be an inheritance for me and my descendants as a reward for following God. The Lord kept me alive till I was eighty-five years old so I could see this day. Give me this hill country, Joshua, where the Anakim live in their fortified cities— and I will drive them out and possess the land."

So Joshua blessed Caleb and gave him the region of Hebron as his inheritance. Reading that story, I can't help thinking that here's Caleb, eighty-five years old, and he's not ready for retirement. He's going to pick up his sword and go right back into the fray! I want to pump iron when I read those words. Caleb had earned the right to play golf or watch TV all day, but that wasn't his way. Caleb is a challenge to all of us who might be tempted to retire from God's work.

A few years ago I went to California's Silicon Valley, south of San Francisco, to speak to a business group. A longtime friend of mine was there, having moved to California from Atlanta. He took me aside and said, "One thing you should know about this audience is that most of them have a certain attitude toward their careers. They think that if they aren't financially independent and retired by age forty-five, they have failed."

"Are you kidding me?" I said. "What do they do with their time?"

"They play golf and manage their investments."

I was flabbergasted. Why would anyone want to be put out to

pasture so early in life? How does anyone derive a meaningful life from knocking a little white ball from hole to hole and shuffling stocks and bonds on a computer screen?

May God give us more Calebs! May God give us more men and women who never give up on the promises of God, who never retire from the work of God, who never waver from their faith in God. This world needs more men and women of faith and optimism who are eager to spend their last breath serving him.

A shoe company once sent a sales representative to open a new foreign office. The man wired a discouraging report: "We can't do business here—no one in this country wears shoes!" The company decided to send a second sales representative to see if the first man was right. The second man wired back, "Send all the shoes you can! The market here is limitless! Everybody here needs shoes!" Both men saw exactly the same conditions, but their reports were like night and day. The difference between them: one man was a pessimist, and the other had an optimistic faith like Caleb's.

If you want to increase your territory, if you want to be blessed by God, if you want to enlarge your opportunities for expanding the kingdom of God, then remember the words of Jesus: "Well done, good and faithful servant. You have been faithful over a little; I will set you over much. Enter into the joy of your master."

Through the eyes of faith

The Church of The Apostles began with thirty-one adults and twenty-one children meeting in a function room at the Waverly Hotel. I had a friend in those days who was a cultural Christian, but in time I had the joy of leading him to the Lord. He owned a lot of real estate. He's with the Lord now, but he once told the church, "I owe Michael Youssef an apology. I used to think, 'Poor Michael—he's a nice fellow, but he's crazy. He's talking about building a three-thousand-seat sanctuary someday!' Now I see what Michael saw through the eyes of faith."

With eyes of optimistic faith, you can see things that do not exist but *will* exist one day. With eyes of optimistic faith, you learn not to despise small beginnings. You learn that if you are faithful with small things, God will trust you with bigger things.

Caleb could have asked Joshua for a golf course and an easy chair. Instead, he asked Joshua for one more hill to climb, one more city to conquer. He said, "Hand me my sword. God has one more job for me to do." Caleb chose to climb the mountain no one else would climb.

Sixteen-year-old Blair Holt loved Air Jordan shoes, rap music, and hanging out with friends. He wrote and recorded music and gave his CDs to friends. Blair was a good student at Julian High School—a happy, big-hearted kid growing up in a tough neighborhood on the South Side of Chicago. His dad was a police officer, his mom a firefighter. His mother dropped him off at school every morning with the words, "Do good, Blair." After school, Blair would board a Chicago Transit Authority bus for a forty-minute ride to his grandparents' grocery store where he clerked and stocked shelves.

One day in May 2007, a tough-looking teenager boarded Blair's bus. As the bus pulled away from the curb, the teen pulled a .40-caliber semiautomatic handgun from his coat, pointed it at another youth on the bus, and started shooting.

Blair was not even in the line of fire, but he saw a girl from school, Tiara Reed, sitting near the gunman. Blair threw himself in front of the girl, shielding her with his body. By the time the gunman had emptied his gun, Blair and four other innocent bystanders were shot. The bus stopped and the gunman got away. So did the youth who was the gunman's target.

Paramedics and police arrived, and an ambulance rushed Blair to the hospital. He was shot through the lungs but conscious, and he told the paramedics to tell his mom and dad he loved them. Blair died that night, about five hours after being shot. It was the Thursday night before Mother's Day, and Blair's mom spent the weekend making funeral arrangements for her only child.

The day before Mother's Day, Tiara Reed visited Blair's mother, Annette Holt, and told her how Blair had saved her life. "Blair is a hero to me," Tiara said. The last morning of Blair Holt's life, his mother had said to him what she always said: "Do good, Blair." He replied, "I will." And later that day, he did.

Someone once said, "You can take the measure of a man by the size of the challenges he undertakes." Blair Holt was a Caleb-sized man. He could have chosen safety. Instead, he chose to do good.

What about you? What about me? What blessings have we left unclaimed because we are afraid of the challenge. Be faithful with the little you've been given. Do good each day, and see how God enlarges your territory. Blair Holt reported for duty at age sixteen; Caleb reported for duty at age eighty-five. Now the Lord wants to know if *you* are ready for action. What will your answer be?

10

Don't Fall Short of
Claiming Your Inheritance

Joshua 15–19

What is the easiest thing in the world to do? *Quit*! It takes no effort to quit. It doesn't cost a dime to quit. Quitting is easy.

Pat Williams, a popular Christian speaker and cofounder of the Orlando Magic, tells about a lesson he learned when he was thirteen years old. He had tried out for a summer baseball league and was chosen to be the youngest player on a team of much older boys. He was plagued by self-doubt and wondered, *What if I'm not good enough to play at the same level as the older players?*

As his mother and grandmother drove him to his first game, Pat told them about his misgivings. Then he added, "Well, if it doesn't work out, I can always quit."

His grandmother whirled around in the front seat, pointed her forefinger in his face, and sternly admonished him, "You don't quit! Nobody in this family quits!"

That thirteen-year-old boy got his grandmother's message loud and clear—and he didn't quit. He later said,

> I've lived by my grandmother's admonition all my life. I don't quit. In 1986, when I was forty-six years old, working eighteen-hour days trying to build the Orlando Magic out of nothing but hopes and dreams, there were many times I wondered, "What have I gotten myself into?" But I never once said to myself, "If it doesn't work out, I can always quit." I truly believe the Orlando Magic would not exist today if it weren't for my sainted grandmother telling me, "You don't quit!"[12]

Perseverance is hard; quitting is easy. If everybody does what comes easy, nothing of significance will ever get accomplished. Without perseverance there would be no inventions, no art, no music, no literature, no sports, no cities, no highways, and no civilization. Nothing worthwhile would ever be achieved if everybody quit at the first sign of adversity or opposition.

Israel never would have been delivered from bondage in Egypt if Moses had quit when things got hard. And Israel never would have possessed the Promised Land if Joshua had quit when things got hard. We would still be lost in our sins if Jesus had quit when things got hard. And the Christian church would not exist today if the apostles had quit when things got hard.

As we come to Joshua 15 through 19, we encounter a series of disturbing statements about God's people. We find they are falling short, they are settling for less than God's best, they are on the verge of quitting. After all that God has brought them through, after all they have accomplished through faith in him, they are about to take the easy way out—and, in the long run, the easy way out is always the hardest way of all.

A record of failure and quitting

First, let's look at Joshua 15 through 17, three chapters that describe the allocation of real estate to the tribes of Judah, Ephraim, and Manasseh. As with some of the previous chapters, I won't quote the full text of this section of Joshua with its detailed descriptions of territories and cities allotted to these three tribes. You can look in your own Bible for the specifics of this division of the land. But note the final verse of Joshua 15:

> But the Jebusites, the inhabitants of Jerusalem, the people of Judah could not drive out, so the Jebusites dwell with the people of Judah at Jerusalem to this day (15:63).

Why did the tribe of Judah fail to drive out the Jebusites? Why did they fall short of carrying out the command of God through Moses and Joshua to completely drive out the pagan people of that land?

The people of Judah stopped short. They quit.

Next, chapters 16 and 17 describe the allotment of real estate for the two tribes of Joseph, the tribes of Ephraim and Manasseh. Here again, at the end of chapter 16, we read these tragic words:

> However, they did not drive out the Canaanites who lived in Gezer, so the Canaanites have lived in the midst of Ephraim to this day but have been made to do forced labor (16:10).

The chapter closes on a note of failure. The tribe of Ephraim quit; they stopped short of carrying out God's command.

Then Joshua 17 describes the allotment for the tribe of Manasseh, Joseph's firstborn. And yet again we read an indictment of failure and quitting:

> Yet the people of Manasseh could not take possession of those cities, but the Canaanites persisted in dwelling in that land. Now when the people of Israel grew strong, they put the Canaanites to forced labor, but did not utterly drive them out (17:12-13).

God didn't tell the Israelites to make slaves of the Canaanites—he said to drive them out. But the people of the tribe of Manasseh quit, and so they were troubled by the Canaanites in their land for generations to come.

There is always a price to be paid when we disobey God's commands.

"How long will you put it off?"

As we come to Joshua 18, we find Joshua in a state of exasperation with his people—and with good reason:

> Then the whole congregation of the people of Israel assembled at Shiloh and set up the tent of meeting there. The land lay subdued before them.
>
> There remained among the people of Israel seven tribes whose inheritance had not yet been apportioned. So Joshua said to the people of Israel, "How long will you put off going in to take possession of the land, which the LORD, the God of your fathers, has given you?" (18:1-3).

"What's wrong with you?" Joshua says to these remaining tribes. "What's taking you so long? What are you waiting for? The Lord has given you this land as an inheritance! Why haven't you claimed it? Why haven't you settled it? Why haven't you developed it?"

God has supernaturally guided the people of Israel. He has led them across the river of impossibility. He has demolished the impenetrable walls of Jericho. He has given them the complete victory, even though their enemies had superior weapons, armor, fortifications, and numbers. The people of Israel have received miracle after miracle from the hand of God.

The hard work is done. The enemies are vanquished. The wars are won. The land is at rest. All that remains is for the tribes of Israel to divide the land among themselves, as Joshua has been doing in previous chapters. The people simply have to pull up in their U-Haul Rent-a-Camel and take possession of the real estate. What could be easier?

Yet they haven't done so. They repeatedly quit before the job is finished. It appears that seven of the tribes have gotten so used to a nomadic lifestyle—a life of wandering the hills and deserts without ever putting down roots—that they are squandering the inheritance God has given them. They have said, in effect, "We've gotten kind of used to driving around the desert in this beat-up Volkswagen bus. Sure, it's cramped and uncomfortable, and the tires are bald and the transmission is shot, but to us, it's home. What would we want with a mansion?"

These Israelites have stubbornly settled for second-best. It's as if they have run a marathon, and have decided to quit after 26 miles and 384 yards—3 feet short of the finish line. Why would anyone come so far and endure so much only to quit when the prize is within their grasp?

Before we criticize the Israelites too harshly, we should recognize that these quitters paint a picture of so many professing Christians. Various surveys have shown that about forty million Americans call themselves evangelicals. The word *evangelical* comes from the Latin word *evangelium*, meaning "good news." So an evangelical should be a person who believes in spreading the good news of faith in Jesus Christ.

If there are truly forty million evangelicals in America, then there should be forty million evangelists daily witnessing and sharing

Christ in their neighborhoods, offices, and schools. There should be waves of conversions sweeping the nation as forty million good news sharers tell everyone they know how to have a personal relationship with Jesus Christ.

Obviously, this is not happening. Instead, the church is anemic and ineffective. Why is that? Why are so many professing Christians today living mediocre lives and having no impact on the world around them? It's because we, like these seven tribes of Israel, have refused to claim our inheritance. We have decided to live in disobedience to God's Word instead of becoming the people God has called us to be. Oh, we still claim to be his children. We go to church on Sundays. When the pollsters ask, we say, "Yes, we're evangelicals. We're professing Christians."

But we don't share the good news with anyone around us. We are so secretive about our Christian faith that our neighbors, our colleagues, and our fellow students have no clue that we are followers of Jesus Christ.

So we are much like those Israelites. We have come so far in our Christian life. We have experienced the miracle of salvation and liberation from guilt and sin. God has brought us over many rivers of impossibility. He has enabled us to conquer addictions, sinful habits, troubled relationships, health problems, depression, and other crises in our lives. He has enabled us to run the marathon of the Christian life—but when the finish line is within reach, we quit.

Some of us are simply embarrassed to tell others about our faith in Christ. God's truth is not trendy and it is not politically correct. It is fashionable today to teach that there are many paths to God, and one path is as good as another. The gospel of Jesus Christ saws across the grain of the fashions and philosophies of this world. Jesus said, "I am the way, and the truth, and the life. No one comes to the Father except through me" (John 14:6). But if you proclaim Jesus as the only way to heaven, you'll be branded "narrow-minded" and "intolerant." So when the subject of religion comes up around the water cooler, we say nothing. We are ashamed of our Lord and his gospel.

The least hint of opposition or ridicule cows us into silence. What if we faced *real* persecution? Many Christians have been martyred for the "crime" of proclaiming Jesus as Lord. Why are we so easily intimidated? I believe it's because quitting is so easy. Why subject ourselves to being laughed at when it is so much easier to quit? We still believe in Jesus Christ, but let's treat his gospel as our little secret.

One of the great tragedies of the church today is that so few Christians have experienced the blessing of sharing their faith and leading others to Christ. One of the greatest experiences we can know is the thrill of leading another human soul into the kingdom. When you witness, and that person responds and asks Jesus to be Lord and Savior, you feel a flutter in your chest and tears of joy in your eyes. Nothing in this world compares with that joy.

The thrill of sharing Christ is part of your inheritance from God. Have you fallen short of your inheritance? God has spread a heavenly feast of joy before you. Why are you living on spiritual food stamps? God has given you the deed to the palace. Why are you settling for a spiritual slum?

Don't forego the blessings of your spiritual inheritance. Don't quit.

Your inheritance: the people around you

Look again at the opening verse of Joshua 18: "Then the whole congregation of the people of Israel assembled at Shiloh and set up the tent of meeting there. The land lay subdued before them." The tent of meeting was Israel's house of worship. Joshua knew that worship was essential to the life of the nation. We need to worship God in order to renew our sense of awe, our obedience, and our motivation to serve him. So when Joshua brought the people together at Shiloh to apportion the rest of their inheritance, he began by calling them to worship.

But Joshua quickly moved from worship to action, as we noted a moment ago (18:2-3). God's ultimate goal for our lives is not that we move into the church but that we move out from the church and into the world. Yes, he wants us to spend regular time in worship with him and fellowship with his people. The problem is that many Christians seem to spend their entire lives in church. They think their mission as Christians is to occupy a certain pew in a certain building every Sunday morning.

My friend, the church is not your mission field. Your mission field starts the moment you walk out the door of your church and onto the street. Your mission field is the neighborhood where you live, the office or factory where you work, the campus where you go to school. God has called you to go out and *conquer the world* in his name! He has called you to go out and *possess the land*.

Worship should challenge, convict, inspire, empower, motivate, revitalize, instruct, and equip you to go out into your mission field and claim your inheritance from the Lord. What is that inheritance? Your inheritance is your God-given territory—your opportunities for witnessing and reaching others for Christ. Your inheritance is the vast circle of people God has placed in your path—your neighbors, coworkers, fellow students, professors, coaches, and all the people who read your blog, Facebook page, Pinterest pinboard, and Twitter messages.

Your inheritance consists of all the people you influence each day. Jesus is knocking at the doors of their hearts. When they open that door a crack, Jesus speaks through you and me as we share his good news.

When Joshua gathered the people at Shiloh to worship the Lord, he did exactly what Christian ministers should do. "Don't let your inheritance go unclaimed," he said. "Don't let God's power and blessing in your life go to waste. Don't let the busyness of this world keep you from your mission field. Don't let the worries and weariness of this world keep you from living as a true apostle for your Lord, wherever you work, live, or play. Don't quit! Conquer the world for Christ!"

We all have social lives, leisure lives, times of relaxing with friends, chatting over coffee, shopping with friends at the mall, exercising with friends at the gym, and on and on. As Christians, our social lives should have a purpose. We should care enough about the people we spend time with to talk to them about truth—and Jesus is the truth. So enjoy your social life and social media, but don't forget to make it count for God.

Nature abhors a vacuum

Joshua was exasperated with the people of Israel. Every day they delayed in taking possession of the land was a day lost in accomplishing God's plan for them. If God's people didn't go out and possess the land, it was only a matter of time before Israel's enemies would return and take the land back. Everything Israel had accomplished through God's power could be lost if the people didn't claim their inheritance.

There is a scientific principle, first expressed by Aristotle in 350 BC: "Nature abhors a vacuum." In other words, an empty space is unnatural because nature will try to fill that space if it can. You can maintain a vacuum in a bottle as long as it is perfectly sealed, but the moment you break that seal, air molecules will rush into the bottle. The vacuum will be replaced by air in seconds.

The same is true in the spiritual realm. Spiritual nature abhors a vacuum. Jesus expressed this principle when he said:

"When the unclean spirit has gone out of a person, it passes through waterless places seeking rest, but finds none. Then it says, 'I will return to my house from which I came.' And when it comes, it finds the house empty, swept, and put in order. Then it goes and brings with it seven other spirits more evil than itself, and they enter and dwell there, and the last state of that person is worse than the first. So also will it be with this evil generation" (Matthew 12:43-45).

Jesus is telling us that when a person comes to him, there is a moment when all of the old evil is cast out of that person's heart. That is the crucial moment when a person must fill his or her life with the Holy Spirit and then keep on being filled. The life of that person must be filled with God, with worship, with Christian fellowship, with Bible study, with witnessing and sharing Christ with others. If that person allows a spiritual vacuum to exist—look out!

I have seen people cry tears of regret because they failed to fill the spiritual vacuum in their lives. They made a commitment to Christ at some point, but they never claimed their inheritance in Christ. As a result, their lives became filled with sin, destructive habits, broken relationships, bitterness, regret, and shame. That's what happens if you fail to claim your inheritance in Christ. That's what happens if you neglect to claim the Lord's power over sin and temptation in your life.

If you leave a spiritual vacuum in your life, it's just a matter of time before your life is reoccupied with the same old sins and habits that plagued you before your conversion. If you do not fill that vacuum with the Lord's Spirit, your heart will ultimately become too hard for God to soften it. That's when evil forces can reoccupy your life and fill you with resentment toward God and resistance to his truth.

I have seen this principle at work in many lives. It's heartbreaking to behold. That's why I appeal to you, as Joshua pleaded with his people: Don't fall short of possessing the territory God has promised you. Don't let one more day go by without claiming your rightful place as the Lord's ambassador, your rightful victory through Christ, and your rightful inheritance in Christ.

The "portion of the sun"

At Joshua's urging, the inheritance of the land of Canaan is finally distributed to the remaining tribes of Israel: Simeon, Zebulun, Issachar, Asher, Naphtali, and Dan. After describing the allotment for each of these tribes, Joshua 19 concludes with these words:

> When they had finished distributing the several territories of the land as inheritances, the people of Israel gave an inheritance among them to Joshua the son of Nun. By command of the LORD they gave him the city that he asked, Timnath-serah in the hill country of Ephraim. And he rebuilt the city and settled in it.
>
> These are the inheritances that Eleazar the priest and Joshua the son of Nun and the heads of the fathers' houses of the tribes of the people of Israel distributed by lot at Shiloh before the LORD, at the entrance of the tent of meeting. So they finished dividing the land (19:49-51).

Joshua, like all great leaders, thought of his people first and himself last. He waited until the other tribes had received their portions before taking his own portion. At the end of the distribution, the people gave Joshua his inheritance—a city called Timnath-serah in the hill country of Ephraim. So Joshua rebuilt the city (perhaps it needed rebuilding after the wars of conquest) and settled there. The name of the city means "portion that remains" or "extra portion." The city was named for the fact that it was the last piece of territory allocated.

This city is mentioned in the book of Judges, but there is a transposition of two Hebrew letters so that it is called Timnath-heres, a name that means "portion of the sun." The Scriptures tell us:

> And Joshua the son of Nun, the servant of the LORD, died at the age of 110 years. And they buried him within the boundaries of his inheritance in Timnath-heres, in the hill country of Ephraim, north of the mountain of Gaash (Judges 2:8-9).

Why was the name of Joshua's city changed from "portion that remains" to "portion of the sun"? The name of the city may have been changed to commemorate the greatest event of Joshua's leadership, the moment when he prayed and God stopped the sun in the sky. A tradition among some Jewish scholars says Joshua's tomb was sealed with a representation of the sun—a symbol commemorating that miraculous event. The present-day site of Joshua's city is unknown, though most scholars identify Timnath-serah with modern Khirbet Tibnah, a Palestinian town in the West Bank, eighteen miles northwest of Jerusalem.

Joshua succeeded in his goal of motivating the Israelite people to claim their inheritance and possess the land God had promised to them. Clearly it was God who parted the waters, God who demolished the walls of Jericho, and God who sent the hailstones and stopped the sun in the sky. But Joshua and his people had to step up, obey, and not quit. They had to claim the inheritance God had promised them.

The crucial lesson of Joshua 15–19 is *don't quit*. Never stop doing the work God has given you. Never stop reaching out to unsaved people with the love of Jesus Christ. Never stop witnessing and spreading the good news. Don't stop short of claiming the precious inheritance God has given you.

You and I are believers today because God pursued us for years until we finally gave our lives to him. He did not give up on us. And we must not quit on him. God has given us a wonderful inheritance, and now it is up to us to claim it.

A champion for God

In the summer of 2012, the whole world was electrified by a four-foot-eleven, ninety-five-pound, sixteen-year-old bundle of gymnastic grace and energy named Gabrielle Douglas. On July 31, at the 2012 London Olympics, she and her USA teammates won the team all-around gold medal. Then, on August 2, Gabby Douglas won the gold medal in the individual all-around event with a heart-stopping performance. In winning the gold, she became the first African-American woman to win the event and the first American gymnast ever to win both the team and individual all-around gold at the same Olympics.[13]

Watching Gabby Douglas's moment of triumph on television, you would never guess how many times she came close to quitting. After her sister Arielle introduced Gabby to gymnastics, she pursued her dream with incredible intensity. From an early age, she would refuse to miss a day of practice even when sick and running a fever. At fourteen, she told her mother she wanted to move twelve hundred miles from her Virginia Beach, Virginia, home to Iowa so she could train with gymnastics coach Liang Chow, who coached Olympic gold medalist Shawn Johnson.

After a few months in Iowa, Gabby became homesick and wanted to quit. She called her mother and said, "I want to come home." It would have been easy for Gabby's mom to say yes to her daughter's plea—but she didn't want Gabby thinking that she could simply quit whenever a challenge became difficult. "Life isn't easy," her mother said. "You have to fight and refuse to quit." So Gabby stayed in Iowa.[14]

Gabby's Olympic year was a difficult one, and again she came close to quitting. She was anxious about her father, who was in Afghanistan with the Air Force (she had not seen him in nearly two years). She told NBC, "I had bad days in the gym, thinking about my dad…I'm just like, 'Whoa, what if he doesn't come back [from the war]?' I was just horrified. I prayed every night."

She struggled in several events leading up to the London Olympics and injured her ankle at the Pacific Rim Championships in March. Shortly before the Olympic Trials in June, Gabby confided to Arielle that she was thinking of quitting and not trying out for the Olympic team. "It was pretty drastic," Arielle later recalled. "She really, really sounded very serious about it."[15]

Arielle talked Gabby into keeping faith with her dream, and Gabby agreed. She went to the Olympic Trials—and heard someone calling her name. She turned and saw her dad in the stands, holding an American flag with Gabby's name written on it. "I almost felt like bawling," she recalled. "I was like, 'Oh, my gosh, Dad!'" Having her dad at the trials lifted Gabby's spirits and elevated her performance. She made the team.

Gabby endured loneliness, homesickness, and physical pain to earn her gold medal. "It took a lot of hard days in the gym," she told a *Today Show* interviewer, "and determination, passion and drive. Gold medals are made out of your sweat, blood and tears, and effort in the gym every day, and sacrificing a lot."[16]

As someone has pointed out, if you rearrange the letters of Gabby Douglas's last name, they spell USA GOLD. She has a strong Christian faith, and she seizes every opportunity to point people to Jesus Christ. After winning her second gold medal in the individual all-around event, she told an NBC reporter, "It definitely is an amazing feeling…And I give all the glory to God. It's kind of a win-win situation. The glory goes up to him and the blessings fall down on me."[17]

One of the ways Gabby expressed her exuberant faith in God is through her Twitter account. On July 28, three days before she and her teammates won gold, she tweeted Joshua 1:9 to thousands of fans: "Have I not commanded you? Be strong and courageous. Do not be afraid; do not be discouraged, for the Lord your God will be with you wherever you go."

On July 30, she tweeted, "I believe in God. He is the secret of my success. He gives people talent." On July 31, the day her team won gold, she quoted the Lord's words in Matthew 6:33: "But seek first the kingdom of God and his righteousness, and all these things will be added to you." And on August 2, the day she won gold in the individual event, she tweeted Psalm 103:2 to her fans: "Let all that I am praise the Lord; may I never forget the good things he does for me."[18]

Though God provided Gabby with talent, she had to step up and say yes to God. She had to suffer and sacrifice for her dream. She had to endure the homesickness and loneliness. She had to spend countless hours on the mat, the parallel bars, and the balance beam. Every time she was tempted to quit, she had to say, "By God's strength, I will keep going."

Do we have the courage and perseverance of this four-foot-eleven, ninety-five-pound teenager? Do we have the faith to be an outspoken witness for Christ? Are we eager to share our testimony at every opportunity? Or do we choose to quit, because quitting is so easy?

Meet resistance with persistence. That's what it takes to be a gold medal champion for God.

11

God's Refugees

Joshua 20

As a boy, I got into my share of mischief. My father was rather long on justice and short on mercy. On those few occasions when I received mercy for my transgressions, it was usually because my mother intervened. When I saw trouble coming, my instinct was to run from my father—as far and as fast as I could.

I'm not saying my father was abusive or unfair. You can be assured that, when he disciplined me, I richly deserved my punishment. Unfortunately, the lessons he tried to teach me never seemed to stick. Temptation always proved stronger than my fear of my father's wrath, so I incurred his wrath with alarming regularity.

During those years, I had a friend who sometimes got into mischief with me. When he got in trouble, he did something that always baffled me: he ran *to* his father, not away from him. It seemed like a totally deranged thing to do! His inexplicable behavior troubled me for a long time.

Only when I committed my life to Christ did I finally understand the difference between his relationship with his father and my relationship with mine. When I became a Christian, I began to develop an intimate relationship with my heavenly Father. I discovered what it means to have a merciful Father. And that's when I understood that my friend's relationship with his father was actually a picture of what our relationship with our heavenly Father is supposed to be.

I've been in the ministry for some forty years, and during that time, I've observed that there are two types of people—those who run *to* their heavenly Father and those who run *from* their heavenly Father. What makes the difference between these two kinds of people? The answer is simple: it all depends on your view of your heavenly Father.

If you view him as a vindictive, arbitrary, angry God who is just waiting to punish you for your sins, you'll run away from him. You won't go to him for forgiveness because you won't expect forgiveness. You will expect punishment. But if you see your heavenly Father as the God of mercy and grace, slow to anger and full of compassion, you will run into his arms for forgiveness.

Unfortunately, many people unconsciously equate their relationship with their heavenly Father with the relationship they've had with their earthly fathers. Those of us who have had harsh and stern earthly fathers often assume that God treats us the same way. Whether your earthly father was gentle or harsh, merciful or stern, don't confuse him with your Father in heaven. The true nature of our heavenly Father is revealed through his Word, and especially through his Son, Jesus, who said, "Whoever has seen me has seen the Father" (John 14:9).

If you want to know what God the Father is like, look at Jesus, who came to earth as fully God and fully Man—the personification of grace and truth. Through him, we know that our heavenly Father loves us and cares for us more than any earthly father could.

As the nineteenth-century minister Henry Ward Beecher once said, "There is no creature so poor or so low, that he may not look up with childlike confidence to the Creator of the universe and exclaim, 'You are my Father!'"

In Joshua 20, we catch a glimpse of yet another facet of the glorious character of our Father in heaven.

Cities of refuge

Throughout the book of Joshua, we've seen how God relates to his people. We've seen God provide in many amazing ways—even stopping the sun in the sky to give them victory over their enemies. Finally, he divided the Land of Promise among the people and mercifully rebuked them when they delayed in claiming their inheritance. Now, in Joshua 20, Israel's merciful heavenly Father instructs the people in how to exercise justice and compassion by designating six cities of refuge.

The cities of refuge were not a new idea the Lord introduced after the Israelites settled in the Promised Land. The first mention of the cities of refuge was in Exodus: "Whoever strikes a man so that he dies shall be put to death. But if he did not lie in wait for him, but God let him fall into his hand, then I will appoint for you a place to which he may flee" (Exodus 21:12-13). The reference to cities of refuge is more detailed and explicit in Numbers:

> And the LORD spoke to Moses, saying, "Speak to the people of Israel and say to them, When you cross the Jordan into the land of Canaan, then you shall select cities to be cities of refuge for you, that the manslayer who kills any person without intent may flee there. The cities shall be for you a refuge from the avenger, that the manslayer may not die until he stands before the congregation for judgment. And the cities that you give shall be your six

cities of refuge. You shall give three cities beyond the Jordan, and three cities in the land of Canaan, to be cities of refuge. These six cities shall be for refuge for the people of Israel, and for the stranger and for the sojourner among them, that anyone who kills any person without intent may flee there" (Numbers 35:9-15).

Another description of the cities of refuge occurs in Deuteronomy 19:1-13. Finally, in Joshua 20, the command to designate cities of refuge is presented again:

Then the LORD said to Joshua, "Say to the people of Israel, 'Appoint the cities of refuge, of which I spoke to you through Moses, that the manslayer who strikes any person without intent or unknowingly may flee there. They shall be for you a refuge from the avenger of blood. He shall flee to one of these cities and shall stand at the entrance of the gate of the city and explain his case to the elders of that city. Then they shall take him into the city and give him a place, and he shall remain with them. And if the avenger of blood pursues him, they shall not give up the manslayer into his hand, because he struck his neighbor unknowingly, and did not hate him in the past. And he shall remain in that city until he has stood before the congregation for judgment, until the death of him who is high priest at the time. Then the manslayer may return to his own town and his own home, to the town from which he fled.'"

So they set apart Kedesh in Galilee in the hill country of Naphtali, and Shechem in the hill country of Ephraim, and Kiriath-arba (that is, Hebron) in the hill country of Judah. And beyond the Jordan east of Jericho, they appointed Bezer in the wilderness on the tableland, from the tribe of Reuben, and Ramoth in Gilead, from the tribe of Gad, and Golan in Bashan, from the tribe of Manasseh. These were the cities designated for all the people of Israel and for the stranger sojourning among them, that anyone who killed a person without intent could flee there, so that he might not die by the hand of the avenger of blood, till he stood before the congregation (20:1-9).

Why does God place so much stress on these cities of refuge? He wants the people of Israel to know that human life is sacred and he desires that his people show mercy. He wants to impress on them the value he places on every human life.

It's a terrible thing to take another human life, and murder shall not be tolerated among God's people. But accidents happen and people are killed unintentionally. God wants his people to understand that there is a difference between intentional murder and unintentional manslaughter. The murderer and the one who committed manslaughter should not be treated the same way.

Hope for the manslayer and the sinner

Capital punishment was instituted under the Law of Moses to underscore the value of human life. Some would see this as contradictory. How can you teach the value of life by killing someone? But looked at another way, the point becomes clear. The law sends a powerful message: the life of your neighbor is so sacred that if you take your neighbor's life by an act of murder, you must pay with your own life.

Unfortunately, human emotion sometimes negates God's law. Two men might be in the forest cutting wood. One man swings his ax, and the ax head flies off, striking and killing the other man. Clearly, there was no murderous intent. This was an accident, and the man who committed unintentional manslaughter should not be put to death for an accident. But the dead man's brother might say, "Accident or not, he killed my brother, and I want revenge!"

So God, who is both the God of justice and the God of mercy, says, "Build six cities throughout Israel—three on the east side of the River Jordan and three on the west. They shall be cities of refuge, and when a man commits manslaughter, he can go to one of those cities and find sanctuary."

God's explicit commands regarding the cities of refuge are given to us through Moses in Exodus, Numbers, and Deuteronomy, and through Joshua in chapter 20. Additionally, the traditions of the rabbis, embodied in the Hebrew writings known as the Talmud, set forth several more requirements. According to Talmudic tradition (which carried great authority in the Jewish culture), the roads to the cities of refuge had to be exceptionally smooth, twice as wide as normal roads, and maintained in excellent condition. The medieval Jewish scholar Maimonides explained the Talmudic teaching this way:

> The court is obligated to straighten the roads to the cities of refuge, to repair them and broaden them. They must remove all impediments and obstacles…[and] bridges should be built (over all natural barriers) so as not to delay one who is fleeing to [the city of refuge]. The width of a road to a city of refuge should not be less than 32 cubits. "Refuge, Refuge" was written at all crossroads so that the perpetrator of manslaughter should recognize the way and turn there.[19]

When the fugitive entered the city, he would be taken to the elders—the legal authority and court of law for the city—to present his case. The elders would likely make a provisional decision to grant asylum to the accused man until a proper trial could be held. If the manslayer was acquitted, he was to live in the city of refuge until the death of the high priest. After the death of the high priest, the manslayer would be free to go home to his community and family, and he could live there in freedom.

At this point, you might say, "I followed God's logic about the cities of refuge until we got to the part about the death of the high priest. Why is the manslayer only freed after the high priest's death?" This aspect of God's command probably baffled the Old Testament Israelites as well. They must have wondered, *What does the death of the high priest have to do with the freedom of the fugitive?*

But with New Testament hindsight, it makes perfect sense. The death of the high priest is the only ransom that can be paid for the act of manslaughter. The death of the high priest was the redemption for the guilt of accidentally taking a human life. The death of the high priest was the atonement for the sin of the fugitive, and the satisfaction for the demands of justice.

Even though the manslayer was not guilty of murder, he was guilty of sin. He had taken an innocent life. Someone was dead because of his unintentional actions. Where there is sin, there is guilt. In order for the fugitive to be free, there must be atonement. At this point, you may already see where God's logic is leading—because his command about the cities of refuge is profoundly meaningful for your life and mine.

You and I are guilty people. We were born guilty because we have inherited the sin of Adam. We are guilty because we have broken the law of God. We are guilty for living only for ourselves while ignoring our righteous and holy God. We are guilty of disobedience and insubordination to our Creator. Whether we have sinned against God out of ignorance or out of deliberate rebellion makes no difference. The courts of heaven have convened and have pronounced us guilty as charged.

But a runner along the way has told us where we can find refuge, relief from guilt and judgment, and escape from our adversary and accuser. So we come to the city of refuge, and there we are set free, not only from sin but from the wages of sin, which is death. And we receive atonement and redemption and complete liberation. Why? Because our Great High Priest has died for us. He has been nailed to a cross on a hill called Calvary.

Once we have been redeemed, we become runners ourselves. We are the ones who point the way to the city of refuge. We are the ones who tell others how to find escape from sin and judgment and everlasting death. We were once refugees. Now God calls us to be runners, leading fugitives to the city of refuge and to the Great High Priest who can set them free.

The death of the Great High Priest has set us free from the curse of sin. There is now no condemnation for us. We have been given new life—eternal life—and God calls us to share this good news with everyone we meet along the way.

The psalmist looked forward to the place of refuge God would provide through the death of the Great High Priest: "God is our refuge and strength, a very present help in trouble" (Psalm 46:1). And while the psalmist looked forward to the death of the Great High Priest, the apostle Paul was able to look back to that same event and say, "There is therefore now no condemnation for those who are in Christ Jesus" (Romans 8:1). And the writer to the Hebrews was able to write that "we who have fled for refuge might have strong encouragement to hold fast to the hope set before us" (Hebrews 6:18).

No one who is in Christ Jesus, who has fled to him for refuge, has anything to fear from the judgment to come. Notice, I did not say you have nothing to fear if you attend church or if you belong to a certain denomination or if you observe certain religious rituals. The only city of refuge we have is the Lord Jesus himself. If you are in Christ, you have refuge. But as long as you remain apart from him, you are under judgment. The good news is that you can go to him for refuge today, at this very moment.

There may be a person who has heard the gospel again and again, but has never gone in repentance to Jesus Christ for mercy, forgiveness, and refuge. As a result, *that person has the most to fear from God's judgment*. He or she is responsible for that truth. Those who have heard the truth but refuse to act on it will be judged more severely than those who have never heard. So don't delay. Urge people to go to Jesus now. Pray for them. Ask God to enter their lives and take over as Savior and Lord. Pray that they seek him now, while he is calling them. Tomorrow might be too late.

The church is not the city of refuge. The church is merely the signpost that calls out, "Flee to Christ! Take refuge in him!" Only when each one flees to Jesus, the Great High Priest who died for them, will they find freedom from guilt and peace in times of trouble.

The poison of sin

When you feel convicted of sin, which way do you run? Do you run *away* from your heavenly Father, as I ran from my father when I was a boy? Or do you run *to* him, seeking refuge and forgiveness? Do you fear his wrath—or long for his mercy? When you have sinned, do you avoid the church and the fellowship of other Christians? Do you fear that the sermon and hymns will make you fear God's judgment? Or do you eagerly go to church to receive a cleansing message of God's mercy and grace?

Do you run *to* your city of refuge—or do you run *away*?

In *A Daily Passage Through Mark*, John R. Wayland tells of the 1981 theft of a Volkswagen Beetle somewhere in California—a story reported on the national news media. Of course, hundreds of cars are stolen every day. Why would the theft of one particular VW Bug become a national news story? Answer: A box of crackers.

The owner of the car had laced the crackers with rat poison and was planning to set the crackers out as bait to kill rodents. After the car was stolen, the owner and the police wanted to apprehend the thief—not merely to recover the car but to save the thief from being poisoned![20]

I don't know if the thief was apprehended—Wayland doesn't tell us in his book. But I do know that many people are like that car thief. They're on the run from God, afraid of his punishment. They do everything possible to elude him, yet all God wants is to rescue them from the poison of sin.

If you have taken refuge in Jesus, and he is your Lord and Savior, I have a question for you: Are you a runner for God? Are you pointing the way for other fugitives so they can find their city of refuge? Every day, you encounter fugitives from God's judgment. They are fearful and exhausted. Their backs are breaking under a load of sin. They are desperate for mercy and forgiveness. You know the way to the city of refuge. Have you told anyone? Or are you keeping the good news all to yourself?

You have friends. You share meals with them. You go to movies and concerts with them. Have you ever told them about the city of refuge? Have you ever shared with them the good news of Jesus Christ? If you have been silent, if you've never pointed the way to refuge and healing, then you have to ask yourself, "What kind of friend am I?"

So which will it be? Will you accept God's call to be a runner along the way, or will you abandon your post? Are you guiding other fugitives to the city of refuge, or have you lost your way? Don't let another moment pass without settling these all-important questions between you and God.

12

A Covenant with God

Joshua 21–24

I magine with me a frightening scenario.

You wake up one morning and there is no dawn. By 9:00 a.m., you look out your window and there is not a ray of sunshine. By noon, you step outside and you see that the world is still as black as midnight.

The hours crawl by. Your neighbors huddle in the streets with candles and flashlights. "What's happening?" they ask. "Where is the sun?" You have no answer—but a chill of dread runs through you. You wonder, *Will the sun ever return?*

By evening, the churches are thronged with frightened people. Some who casually blasphemed God's name yesterday now cry out to him, pleading with him to return the sun to the sky. And you are there with the rest of them, praying and wondering if this is the final judgment.

The dark day passes into another dark night. Hours crawl by. After an all-night prayer meeting, you walk out into the street and check your watch. It's 5:30 a.m. You think, *On a normal day, the sun would be coming up soon.*

You look to the east…and you see a faint smudge of light over the horizon. You stare at the eastern sky until you are sure. Yes, you definitely see a few rays of sunlight over the horizon. A new day is dawning.

You turn to the other people as they emerge from the church and you shout, "The sun is rising! The sun is rising!"

Shouts of joy and praise fill the air. People come out of their homes and fill the streets as the sky turns from black to indigo to blue. Your neighbors turn their faces to the sun. After twenty-four hours of darkness and dread, everyone around you gives praise to God. It's morning and the sun has risen.

Now let me ask you a question: Why don't we praise God every single day for the sun? Why don't we feel excited and elated just to awaken each morning to a new day? Why don't we have an attitude of grateful praise every day for the blessings of God's creation?

Because we take God and his gifts for granted. We don't truly appreciate what we have until we lose it. We are a forgetful people.

Spiritual amnesia

God knows we are forgetful by nature. That's why he tells us repeatedly in his Word, "Remember!" Again and again in the Old Testament, God commands us to remember.

> "You shall remember that you were a slave in the land of Egypt, and the LORD your God brought you out from there with a mighty hand and an outstretched arm" (Deuteronomy 5:15).

> "You shall remember the LORD your God, for it is he who gives you power to get wealth" (Deuteronomy 8:18).

"Remember this and stand firm,
  recall it to mind, you transgressors,
  remember the former things of old;
for I am God, and there is no other;
  I am God, and there is none like me."
                                        (Isaiah 46:9)

"Remember the law of my servant Moses, the statutes
and rules that I commanded him at Horeb for all Israel"
(Malachi 4:4).

And again and again in the New Testament, his message is the same:

"Remember the word that I said to you: 'A servant is not
greater than his master'" (John 15:20).

Remember that you were at that time separated from
Christ, alienated from the commonwealth of Israel and
strangers to the covenants of promise, having no hope
and without God in the world (Ephesians 2:12).

"Remember therefore from where you have fallen; repent,
and do the works you did at first" (Revelation 2:5).

Remember, remember! God calls us to awaken from our spiritual amnesia. The medical condition known as amnesia involves a loss of memory, often caused by brain damage due to disease, trauma, or drugs. The amnesia sufferer may forget significant details about his life for hours or years or even for life. An amnesia sufferer often can't recall important milestones in his life, such as the birth of a child or a wedding day, and may even forget his identity.

Spiritual amnesia is far more common than physical amnesia. Spiritual amnesia occurs when we forget the Lord's blessings and mercies. It happens when we allow our present troubles and afflictions to blot out our memory of God's goodness and grace. God knows we are spiritual amnesiacs. He knows we are prone to taking his blessings for granted. That's why, in the closing pages of Joshua, he says, in effect, "Don't forget what I've done for you. Don't be ungrateful. Remember me."

The significance of Shechem

In preceding chapters, we have seen the nation of Israel finally taking possession of the land and dividing it among the tribes, then designating cities of refuge. Now, in Joshua 21, the Israelites set aside cities for the priests of the Levite tribe:

> Then the heads of the fathers' houses of the Levites came to Eleazar the priest and to Joshua the son of Nun and to the heads of the fathers' houses of the tribes of the people of Israel. And they said to them at Shiloh in the land of Canaan, "The LORD commanded through Moses that we be given cities to dwell in, along with their pasturelands for our livestock." So by command of the LORD the people of Israel gave to the Levites the following cities and pasturelands out of their inheritance (21:1-3).

After detailed descriptions of the towns and pasturelands allotted to the Levites, chapter 21 closes with a statement that Israel now enjoys peace and prosperity in fulfillment of the promise God made to the nation:

> Thus the LORD gave to Israel all the land that he swore to give to their fathers. And they took possession of it, and they settled there. And the LORD gave them rest on every side just as he had sworn to their fathers. Not one of all their enemies had withstood them, for the LORD had

given all their enemies into their hands. Not one word of all the good promises that the LORD had made to the house of Israel had failed; all came to pass (21:43-45).

This is a powerful statement, and one that is reassuring to our faith today. God has kept all of his promises to Israel; not a single promise of God has failed. And God will keep his promises to us as well.

The unity of the Spirit in the bond of peace

In Joshua 22, Joshua blesses the tribes who had chosen to settle on the east side of the Jordan River—the Reubenites, the Gadites, and the half-tribe of Manasseh. This chapter also records a misunderstanding over an altar that these eastern tribes had built, and how that misunderstanding was peacefully resolved.

> At that time Joshua summoned the Reubenites and the Gadites and the half-tribe of Manasseh, and said to them, "You have kept all that Moses the servant of the LORD commanded you and have obeyed my voice in all that I have commanded you. You have not forsaken your brothers these many days, down to this day, but have been careful to keep the charge of the LORD your God. And now the LORD your God has given rest to your brothers, as he promised them. Therefore turn and go to your tents in the land where your possession lies, which Moses the servant of the LORD gave you on the other side of the Jordan. Only be very careful to observe the commandment and the law that Moses the servant of the LORD commanded you, to love the LORD your God, and to walk in all his ways and to keep his commandments and to cling to him and to serve him with all your heart and with all your soul." So Joshua blessed them and sent them away, and they went to their tents.

Now to the one half of the tribe of Manasseh Moses had given a possession in Bashan, but to the other half Joshua had given a possession beside their brothers in the land west of the Jordan. And when Joshua sent them away to their homes and blessed them, he said to them, "Go back to your tents with much wealth and with very much livestock, with silver, gold, bronze, and iron, and with much clothing. Divide the spoil of your enemies with your brothers." So the people of Reuben and the people of Gad and the half-tribe of Manasseh returned home, parting from the people of Israel at Shiloh, which is in the land of Canaan, to go to the land of Gilead, their own land of which they had possessed themselves by command of the LORD through Moses.

And when they came to the region of the Jordan that is in the land of Canaan, the people of Reuben and the people of Gad and the half-tribe of Manasseh built there an altar by the Jordan, an altar of imposing size. And the people of Israel heard it said, "Behold, the people of Reuben and the people of Gad and the half-tribe of Manasseh have built the altar at the frontier of the land of Canaan, in the region about the Jordan, on the side that belongs to the people of Israel." And when the people of Israel heard of it, the whole assembly of the people of Israel gathered at Shiloh to make war against them.

Then the people of Israel sent to the people of Reuben and the people of Gad and the half-tribe of Manasseh, in the land of Gilead, Phinehas the son of Eleazar the priest, and with him ten chiefs, one from each of the tribal families of Israel, every one of them the head of a family among the clans of Israel. And they came to the people of Reuben, the people of Gad, and the half-tribe of Manasseh, in the land of Gilead, and they said to them, "Thus says the whole congregation of the LORD, 'What is this breach of faith that you have committed against the God of Israel in

turning away this day from following the LORD by building
yourselves an altar this day in rebellion against the LORD?
Have we not had enough of the sin at Peor from which
even yet we have not cleansed ourselves, and for which
there came a plague upon the congregation of the LORD,
that you too must turn away this day from following the
LORD? And if you too rebel against the LORD today then
tomorrow he will be angry with the whole congregation
of Israel. But now, if the land of your possession is unclean,
pass over into the LORD's land where the LORD's tabernacle stands, and take for yourselves a possession among us.
Only do not rebel against the LORD or make us as rebels
by building for yourselves an altar other than the altar of
the LORD our God. Did not Achan the son of Zerah break
faith in the matter of the devoted things, and wrath fell
upon all the congregation of Israel? And he did not perish
alone for his iniquity.'"

Then the people of Reuben, the people of Gad, and
the half-tribe of Manasseh said in answer to the heads of
the families of Israel, "The Mighty One, God, the LORD!
The Mighty One, God, the LORD! He knows; and let Israel
itself know! If it was in rebellion or in breach of faith against
the LORD, do not spare us today for building an altar to
turn away from following the LORD. Or if we did so to
offer burnt offerings or grain offerings or peace offerings
on it, may the LORD himself take vengeance. No, but we
did it from fear that in time to come your children might
say to our children, 'What have you to do with the LORD,
the God of Israel? For the LORD has made the Jordan a
boundary between us and you, you people of Reuben
and people of Gad. You have no portion in the LORD.' So
your children might make our children cease to worship
the LORD. Therefore we said, 'Let us now build an altar,
not for burnt offering, nor for sacrifice, but to be a witness between us and you, and between our generations

after us, that we do perform the service of the LORD in his presence with our burnt offerings and sacrifices and peace offerings, so your children will not say to our children in time to come, "You have no portion in the LORD."' And we thought, 'If this should be said to us or to our descendants in time to come, we should say, "Behold, the copy of the altar of the LORD, which our fathers made, not for burnt offerings, nor for sacrifice, but to be a witness between us and you."' Far be it from us that we should rebel against the LORD and turn away this day from following the LORD by building an altar for burnt offering, grain offering, or sacrifice, other than the altar of the LORD our God that stands before his tabernacle!"

When Phinehas the priest and the chiefs of the congregation, the heads of the families of Israel who were with him, heard the words that the people of Reuben and the people of Gad and the people of Manasseh spoke, it was good in their eyes. And Phinehas the son of Eleazar the priest said to the people of Reuben and the people of Gad and the people of Manasseh, "Today we know that the LORD is in our midst, because you have not committed this breach of faith against the LORD. Now you have delivered the people of Israel from the hand of the LORD."

Then Phinehas the son of Eleazar the priest, and the chiefs, returned from the people of Reuben and the people of Gad in the land of Gilead to the land of Canaan, to the people of Israel, and brought back word to them. And the report was good in the eyes of the people of Israel. And the people of Israel blessed God and spoke no more of making war against them to destroy the land where the people of Reuben and the people of Gad were settled. The people of Reuben and the people of Gad called the altar Witness, "For," they said, "it is a witness between us that the LORD is God" (22:1-34).

A misunderstanding had arisen. The tribes in the land of Gilead east of the Jordan—Reuben and Gad and the half-tribe of Manasseh—had built an altar in violation of God's law. The only altar of worship and sacrifice permitted was the altar that stood before God's tabernacle. So the other tribes sent a delegation, led by Phinehas the son of Eleazar the priest, to confront the problem.

Their message, in essence, was: "You are breaking God's law! You are rebelling against the Lord! You are going to bring judgment on us all! Don't you remember the plague we suffered when the prophet Balaam made sacrifices to God on a Moabite altar on the mountain in Peor? [See Numbers 25.] And remember how we all suffered the consequences when Achan stole from the plunder at Jericho? [See Joshua 7.]"

It turned out, however, that the tribes of Reuben, Gad, and Manasseh had no intention of making sacrifices on the altar they had built. The altar was intended solely as a memorial, a reminder, not a site of worship. These tribes understood that it was unlawful to make sacrifices anywhere but at the altar in front of the tabernacle. But they wanted a "copy of the altar of the LORD...not for burnt offerings, nor for sacrifice, but to be a witness between us and you."

Phinehas and the rest of the delegation listened with an open mind, and then they accepted the explanation. Phinehas replied, "Today we know that the LORD is in our midst, because you have not committed this breach of faith against the LORD. Now you have delivered the people of Israel from the hand of the LORD."

Here we see how disputes within the family of faith should be handled. Both sides should be committed to peace and brotherhood. Each side should listen to the other with an open mind and an open heart. Both sides should avoid casting blame or attacking motives. And both sides should be willing to believe the best about the other and not assume the worst. If only Christians today would learn from the example of Israel and see what it means (as the apostle Paul put it) to "maintain the unity of the Spirit in the bond of peace" (Ephesians 4:3).

A reminder—and a warning

Then in Joshua 23, the old warrior sees that the end of his life is approaching. Joshua summons the leaders of Israel—the elders, judges, and officials of the tribes—and he reminds them of all that God has done for them:

> A long time afterward, when the LORD had given rest to Israel from all their surrounding enemies, and Joshua was old and well advanced in years, Joshua summoned all Israel, its elders and heads, its judges and officers, and said to them, "I am now old and well advanced in years. And you have seen all that the LORD your God has done to all these nations for your sake, for it is the LORD your God who has fought for you. Behold, I have allotted to you as an inheritance for your tribes those nations that remain, along with all the nations that I have already cut off, from the Jordan to the Great Sea in the west. The LORD your God will push them back before you and drive them out of your sight. And you shall possess their land, just as the LORD your God promised you. Therefore, be very strong to keep and to do all that is written in the Book of the Law of Moses, turning aside from it neither to the right hand nor to the left, that you may not mix with these nations remaining among you or make mention of the names of their gods or swear by them or serve them or bow down to them, but you shall cling to the LORD your God just as you have done to this day. For the LORD has driven out before you great and strong nations. And as for you, no man has been able to stand before you to this day. One man of you puts to flight a thousand, since it is the LORD

your God who fights for you, just as he promised you. Be very careful, therefore, to love the LORD your God. For if you turn back and cling to the remnant of these nations remaining among you and make marriages with them, so that you associate with them and they with you, know for certain that the LORD your God will no longer drive out these nations before you, but they shall be a snare and a trap for you, a whip on your sides and thorns in your eyes, until you perish from off this good ground that the LORD your God has given you.

"And now I am about to go the way of all the earth, and you know in your hearts and souls, all of you, that not one word has failed of all the good things that the LORD your God promised concerning you. All have come to pass for you; not one of them has failed. But just as all the good things that the LORD your God promised concerning you have been fulfilled for you, so the LORD will bring upon you all the evil things, until he has destroyed you from off this good land that the LORD your God has given you, if you transgress the covenant of the LORD your God, which he commanded you, and go and serve other gods and bow down to them. Then the anger of the LORD will be kindled against you, and you shall perish quickly from off the good land that he has given to you" (23:1-16).

With the end of his life approaching, Joshua reminds Israel's leaders of the goodness of God and of the fulfillment of all his promises: "And you have seen all that the LORD your God has done to all these nations for your sake, for it is the LORD your God who has fought for you."

But Joshua also warns Israel of the terrible consequences if the people ever turn away from God to serve false gods. "Just as all the good things that the LORD your God promised concerning you have been fulfilled for you," he tells them, "so the LORD will bring upon you all the evil things…if you transgress the covenant of the LORD your God, which he commanded you, and go and serve other gods."

A monument of remembrance

Next, in Joshua 24, the last chapter of the book, Joshua assembles all the tribes of Israel at a place called Shechem, where (according to tradition) the Palestinian village of Nablus stands today. Six centuries earlier, the Lord had appeared to Abraham at Shechem, and there he confirmed his promise to give the land of Canaan to Abraham's descendants. So Joshua deliberately chose Shechem as the meeting place because of its historical significance to the Hebrew people.

Six hundred years is a long time to us, but scarcely a tick of the clock to the Creator of the universe. Human beings might forget a promise made six centuries earlier, but God never forgets. The promise was confirmed to Abraham at Shechem; there a grateful Abraham built an altar of worship to the Lord (see Genesis 12:6-7). And it was at Shechem that Jacob, Abraham's grandson, ordered his entire household to surrender their hidden idols so they could worship the one true God. Jacob buried the idols at the base of a tree in Shechem (see Genesis 35:4). So Joshua assembled the tribes of Israel at a place of deep spiritual and cultural significance, a place of remembrance.

> Joshua gathered all the tribes of Israel to Shechem and summoned the elders, the heads, the judges, and the officers of Israel. And they presented themselves before God. And Joshua said to all the people, "Thus says the LORD, the God of Israel, 'Long ago, your fathers lived beyond the Euphrates, Terah, the father of Abraham and of Nahor; and they served other gods. Then I took your father Abraham from beyond the River and led him through all the land of Canaan, and made his offspring many. I gave him Isaac. And to Isaac I gave Jacob and Esau. And I gave Esau

the hill country of Seir to possess, but Jacob and his children went down to Egypt. And I sent Moses and Aaron, and I plagued Egypt with what I did in the midst of it, and afterward I brought you out.

"'Then I brought your fathers out of Egypt, and you came to the sea. And the Egyptians pursued your fathers with chariots and horsemen to the Red Sea. And when they cried to the LORD, he put darkness between you and the Egyptians and made the sea come upon them and cover them; and your eyes saw what I did in Egypt. And you lived in the wilderness a long time. Then I brought you to the land of the Amorites, who lived on the other side of the Jordan. They fought with you, and I gave them into your hand, and you took possession of their land, and I destroyed them before you. Then Balak the son of Zippor, king of Moab, arose and fought against Israel. And he sent and invited Balaam the son of Beor to curse you, but I would not listen to Balaam. Indeed, he blessed you. So I delivered you out of his hand. And you went over the Jordan and came to Jericho, and the leaders of Jericho fought against you, and also the Amorites, the Perizzites, the Canaanites, the Hittites, the Girgashites, the Hivites, and the Jebusites. And I gave them into your hand. And I sent the hornet before you, which drove them out before you, the two kings of the Amorites; it was not by your sword or by your bow. I gave you a land on which you had not labored and cities that you had not built, and you dwell in them. You eat the fruit of vineyards and olive orchards that you did not plant'" (24:1-13).

Joshua gathered Israel at that site to remind the people of the faithfulness of God—the God who never forgets his promises, the God who always keeps his word. And Joshua reminded the people of God's goodness to Israel, year after year, century after century.

He began by reminding them that God called Abraham out from among the tribes of idol worshipers who lived beyond the Euphrates River. God brought Abraham into Canaan and gave him many descendants—Isaac, Jacob, and the children of Jacob who went down into Egypt.

Then Joshua reminded the people how God had used Moses and Aaron to deliver Israel out of Egypt; how God had vanquished the Egyptians and led the people through the Red Sea and provided for them in the desert; how God gave them victory over the Canaanites and Amorites and all their many enemies in the land. These victories were not won by the sword and bow of the Israelites but by the supernatural might of the Lord.

Then Joshua reminded the people that God had given them a land on which they had not toiled, cities they had not built, and produce from vineyards and olive groves they had not planted. Everything they had was a gift of God's grace. Joshua gave them one reminder after another of God's rich blessing in their lives—and he did so at this historical site called Shechem, Israel's monument of remembrance.

We all need a Shechem in our lives. Your Shechem may be a place in your mind, a monument in your memory, or it may be a geographical site—the place where God met you in a special way and transformed your life. It's the place where God gave us grace far beyond anything we deserved. We all need a Shechem, a place where we can go to remember the goodness and faithfulness of God.

Joshua's exasperation

Next, in verses 14 through 28, we encounter a section that is surprising, even a bit troubling. It seems that, as Joshua reminds the people of all that God has done for them, their response is tepid and lacking in enthusiasm. If you have ever spoken in public, you know how easy it is to read the emotions of an audience. You can tell whether people are responding to your words or zoning out. As you read through the next few verses, you get the impression that Joshua's audience was lukewarm at best. Joshua says:

> "Now therefore fear the LORD and serve him in sincerity and in faithfulness. Put away the gods that your fathers served beyond the River and in Egypt, and serve the LORD. And if it is evil in your eyes to serve the LORD, choose this day whom you will serve, whether the gods your fathers served in the region beyond the River, or the gods of the Amorites in whose land you dwell. But as for me and my house, we will serve the LORD."
>
> Then the people answered, "Far be it from us that we should forsake the LORD to serve other gods, for it is the LORD our God who brought us and our fathers up from the land of Egypt, out of the house of slavery, and who did those great signs in our sight and preserved us in all the way that we went, and among all the peoples through whom we passed. And the LORD drove out before us all the peoples, the Amorites who lived in the land. Therefore we also will serve the LORD, for he is our God."
>
> But Joshua said to the people, "You are not able to serve the LORD, for he is a holy God. He is a jealous God; he will not forgive your transgressions or your sins. If you forsake the LORD and serve foreign gods, then he will turn and do you harm and consume you, after having done you good." And the people said to Joshua, "No, but we will serve the LORD." Then Joshua said to the people, "You are witnesses against yourselves that you have chosen the LORD, to serve him." And they said, "We are witnesses." He said, "Then put away the foreign gods that are among you, and incline your heart to the LORD, the God of Israel." And the people said to Joshua, "The LORD our God we will serve, and his voice we will obey" (24:14-24).

As Joshua spoke to the people, he watched their expressions and body language. Some were yawning or scratching their necks. Some were talking among themselves. Joshua could read these people like a book. He knew what they were thinking. He could see it on their faces—a look that said, "Huh? Oh, yeah, we heard you. Yes, we'll serve the Lord, Joshua. Whatever you say."

After this lukewarm response, Joshua got a little hot under the collar. He demanded that the people make a decision: "Choose this day whom you will serve, whether the gods your fathers served in the region beyond the River, or the gods of the Amorites in whose land you dwell. But as for me and my house, we will serve the Lord" (24:15).

This challenge stirred the people. They realized that Joshua meant business—and he wasn't pleased with their tepid response. So they said, "Far be it from us that we should forsake the Lord to serve other gods...Therefore we also will serve the Lord, for he is our God" (24:16,18).

But Joshua still wasn't satisfied. He clearly believed that the people weren't responding with genuine conviction, so he openly expressed his doubts about the seriousness of their commitment. "You are not able to serve the Lord," Joshua told them, "for he is a holy God. He is a jealous God; he will not forgive your transgressions or your sins. If you forsake the Lord and serve foreign gods, then he will turn and do you harm and consume you, after having done you good" (24:19-20).

The people responded even more vehemently: "No, but we will serve the Lord" (24:21).

Why was Joshua so hard on them? Why was he so skeptical? Why did he say, "You are not able to serve the Lord"?

I believe Joshua wanted to impress the people with the seriousness of this commitment. He was saying, "Don't just worship

Jehovah half-heartedly. Don't serve him out of a sense of obligation. Don't think you can bribe him to get him on your good side. Don't just go through the motions of being religious while your heart is set on the things of this world."

Joshua knew that people are prone to spiritual amnesia, so he drove the point home with a sledgehammer: "You say you're going to serve God. Well, your response doesn't inspire my confidence. Maybe you'll keep this covenant and maybe you won't. Maybe you'll persevere in serving the Lord—or maybe you'll forget your promise and go off after other gods. You are responsible for your own choices, but as far as our family is concerned, we will serve the Lord."

Joshua didn't care about peer pressure. He didn't care if other people mocked and ridiculed him. He wanted nothing to do with half-hearted commitments. "But as for me and my house," he said with conviction, "we will serve the LORD."

The danger of idolatry

Why was Joshua worried that the Israelites would worship idols? After seeing so many miraculous displays of God's power, how could they ever put their trust in idols of stone or brass? Did Joshua seriously think the nation of Israel would turn away from God? Yes, that's exactly what he thought.

He knew the people were prone to spiritual amnesia because they had lapsed into idolatry before. They had been miraculously delivered from bondage in Egypt, had fed on manna in the wilderness, were led through the desert by a pillar of cloud and a pillar of fire—yet in no time at all, they turned from God and worshipped a golden calf!

The sin of idolatry is still a danger in our lives today. We Christians have our idols that seduce our hearts away from God. You may not know my idols, and I don't know yours, but we all have them.

Joshua is speaking not merely to the Israelites gathered at Shechem. He also speaks across the centuries to your heart and mine. He is trying to shake us out of our moral smugness and spiritual amnesia. He is shouting to us, "You are not able to serve the Lord! He is a holy God, a jealous God! Don't worship him half-heartedly! Don't just go through the motions of being religious while your heart is far from God!"

As the apostle Paul tells us,

> For [God] says,
> "In a favorable time I listened to you,
>   and in a day of salvation I have helped you."
> Behold, now is the favorable time; behold, now is the
>   day of salvation.
>
> (2 Corinthians 6:2)

So make your commitment—*now*. Take a stand for Christ—*now*. Let your walk match your talk—*now*. Not tomorrow. Not one of these days. *Now*. You can't even take your next breath, your next heartbeat for granted. You woke up this morning, and God granted you one more day, but there's no guarantee you'll wake up tomorrow.

There's a reason God gave this day to you, so ask him, *Lord, how can I serve you today? Who have you placed in my path today? Who do you want me to talk to today? Who needs to hear the good news today?* Ask God these questions every day, and you'll be amazed at the answers he gives you.

A.B. Earle was an evangelist in nineteenth-century America. Converted to Christ at age sixteen, he became a preacher at eighteen and had a six-decade-long career preaching for the Lord. Once, while preaching in Connecticut, Earle saw one of the state's most prominent attorneys come into the evangelistic service. The man was wealthy and famous, but he didn't have God in his life.

As Earle gave the gospel message, he felt God calling him to do something out of the ordinary. "Usually," he told the audience, "I invite people to leave their chairs and come forward so I can pray with them to receive Christ. But tonight, instead of coming forward, I want you to get out of your chair and kneel on the floor. Let the act of kneeling before God be the visible symbol of the covenant you make with him. Let it be the token of your surrender to God—a surrender you will never take back. But kneel only if you intend to make a covenant of total surrender to him."

As Earle said these words, he saw the attorney shift in his chair and move as if to kneel—then he sat back. Then he moved again toward the floor. The whole time he was lowering himself toward the floor, something seemed to strive inside him for control of his body, preventing his knees from touching the floor.

Then—at last!—the man was on his knees. Instantly, the struggle ceased.

Earle said the man later told him that "the moment his knee reached the floor, he felt the witness in his heart that he was born again. This action of the will unbolted the door of the heart so that the Spirit entered and imparted life" to the attorney.[21]

If you are holding anything back from God, if any idol in your life has stolen your affection for the Lord Jesus, I urge you to surrender your will to him now. Unbolt the door of your heart and invite him in. His Spirit will enter and impart life to you—eternal life through Jesus Christ.

A covenant with God

The people of Israel unbolted their hearts and declared their commitment to Joshua: "The LORD our God we will serve, and his voice we will obey." The Scriptures tell us what Joshua did next:

> So Joshua made a covenant with the people that day, and put in place statutes and rules for them at Shechem. And Joshua wrote these words in the Book of the Law of God. And he took a large stone and set it up there under the terebinth that was by the sanctuary of the LORD. And Joshua said to all the people, "Behold, this stone shall be a witness against us, for it has heard all the words of the LORD that he spoke to us. Therefore it shall be a witness against you, lest you deal falsely with your God." So Joshua sent the people away, every man to his inheritance (24:25-28).

The people of Israel confirmed their covenant with the Lord, and Joshua erected a large stone as a memorial and a witness to the covenant they had made. Then he sent the people back to their homes, "every man to his inheritance." And soon afterward, Joshua himself went to his own inheritance:

> After these things Joshua the son of Nun, the servant of the LORD, died, being 110 years old. And they buried him in his own inheritance at Timnath-serah, which is in the hill country of Ephraim, north of the mountain of Gaash.
>
> Israel served the LORD all the days of Joshua, and all the days of the elders who outlived Joshua and had known all the work that the LORD did for Israel.
>
> As for the bones of Joseph, which the people of Israel brought up from Egypt, they buried them at Shechem, in the piece of land that Jacob bought from the sons of Hamor the father of Shechem for a hundred pieces of money. It became an inheritance of the descendants of Joseph.
>
> And Eleazar the son of Aaron died, and they buried him at Gibeah, the town of Phinehas his son, which had been given him in the hill country of Ephraim (24:29-33).

What a great inheritance Joshua had! And what a legacy he left for you and me. Born a slave in Egypt, he died an honored leader of a nation. Joshua was a man of optimistic faith who followed his Lord across the river of impossibility into the Land of Promise. By faith, he saw the walls of Jericho topple to the ground. By faith, he saw the land of Canaan delivered from idolatry. By faith, he saw God stop the sun in its tracks. By faith, he led the people of Israel into a covenant relationship with the Lord.

Our God is a covenant-making, covenant-keeping God. He never forgets his promises. He fulfills every one. And the greatest promise of all is the promise of the Lord Jesus at the conclusion of Matthew's gospel:

> "All authority in heaven and on earth has been given to me. Go therefore and make disciples of all nations, baptizing them in the name of the Father and of the Son and of the Holy Spirit, teaching them to observe all that I have commanded you. And behold, *I am with you always*, to the end of the age" (Matthew 28:18-20, emphasis added).

Throughout Joshua 24, God reminds his people of his presence, his provision, his deliverance. He took them out of the mud pits of Egyptian slavery, led them through the depths of the Red Sea, fed them manna in the wilderness, brought them safely across the River Jordan, and gave them victory after victory over all their enemies. Again and again in this passage, God reminds the people of what he has done in their lives: "I took your father Abraham...I brought you out...I gave [the enemy] into your hand...I brought you to the land...I gave you a land...I delivered you."

The Lord has the same reminder for you and me. He provides strength and health. He gives us the ability to earn a living. He gives us our talents and abilities. He provides the ability to think and make decisions. He places us in a land brimming with opportunities. He delivers us from illness and injury. Even the children we love so much are God's gift to us, and we are temporary stewards of those gifts. Everything we enjoy in life is a gift and a blessing from God. What is our response to all of his blessings?

Once, while I was on a book tour in Dallas, a TV interviewer said to me, "You've written a book about an Old Testament character who took a stand for God, and God blessed him and used him in a miraculous way. But that's an old story from the Bible. Things like that don't happen anymore, do they?"

I replied, "You have just introduced me as someone who is broadcasting the gospel around the world twenty-three hundred times a week. Well, normally I don't like to talk about myself, but I will do so now for the glory of God. You are looking at a man who should not be here, except for the grace of God. Before I was born, my mother had serious health problems, and the doctor decided I should be aborted. It was only a miracle of God that enabled me to live.

"I grew up in Egypt where I was raised in a Christian home surrounded by a Muslim culture. Even though I didn't always behave like a Christian, my first name, Michael, marked me as coming from a Christian family. So, during the first nineteen years of my life, I grew up knowing what it feels like to be persecuted for Christ.

"I had low self-esteem as a young man. I didn't think I had any talents or abilities. I certainly had no writing or speaking skills. At age twenty, I couldn't even put two sentences together. When I was twenty-two, I took pen and paper and made a list of my assets and liabilities. The list of my flaws and defects wouldn't fit on a single page. As for my skills and talents—that page was blank. I couldn't think of one! I was painfully shy. I saw myself as a nobody with nothing to offer God.

"But I said to Jesus, 'Lord, I know you died on the cross for me. I know you saved me from the wages of sin. You gave me your all, and I have nothing to give to you. All I have to give you is my all, which is next to nothing. Use me in any way you choose.'

"And today, twenty-three hundred times a week, the gospel of Jesus Christ is broadcast to millions of people in more than 190 countries. God took all that I am, which is next to nothing, and he did something extraordinary. You don't think God still uses people the way he did in the Old Testament? I stand here as living proof that he does."

A long time ago, I made an amazing discovery: God is not looking for *ability*. He's looking for *availability*. God wants us to offer him our all—even if our all is nearly a zero. We need to continually remind ourselves of our gratitude to God for all the good things he has done for us, and the best way to demonstrate our gratitude is by living our lives for him. God has blessed us richly so that we may become his witnesses and ambassadors.

When Jesus came down from heaven, he came as one of us. He came as a baby. He grew up as a man, vulnerable to all the hurts, sorrows, and dangers that afflict us all. He allowed himself to be nailed to a cross. He allowed his blood to be spilled. He paid the highest price imaginable to purchase our redemption—a price of suffering and shame, a price of separation from the Father, a price of darkness and death.

What is our response? Shall we simply say, "Thank you, Jesus," then go on with our selfish, materialistic lives? Or should our response be costly as well? If we are truly grateful to God for all he has done for us, shouldn't it cost us something to show our gratitude? Shouldn't it cost us all that we have and all that we are?

What is your river of impossibility? What is the formidable, intimidating Jericho in your life? What is the setback at Ai that leaves you feeling betrayed and defeated? What is the Gibeonite deception that left you feeling foolish and in desperate need of God's wisdom? What battles are you facing right now? What is the miracle you need right now? What lands do you need to conquer? What inheritance have you left unclaimed? Do you need to find a place of refuge? Is there someone in your life who needs your help to find a place of refuge?

The wisdom, courage, and strength you need for all these challenges can be found in the book of Joshua. So be strong and courageous, my friend. Do not be frightened and do not be dismayed.

The Lord your God is with you wherever you go.

Notes

1. Richard Niebuhr, *The Kingdom of God in America* (New York: Harper and Row Publishers, 1937), 193.

2. George G. Hunter III, *The Celtic Way of Evangelism: How Christianity Can Reach the West...Again* (Nashville: Abingdon Press, 2000), 9.

3. C.S. Lewis, *Mere Christianity* (New York: Macmillan, 1960), 51.

4. Mitsuo Fuchida, "The Enemy Whose Attack Provoked America," http://www.christianity.com/ChurchHistory/11635054/.

5. For more information on how God used the author to cross many rivers of impossibility, read Michael Youssef, *Trust and Obey: A Story of God's Faithfulness* (Atlanta: Kobri Books, 2012).

6. George Verwer, *Hunger for Reality / Revolution of Love* (CrownHill, Milton Keynes, UK: Authentic Media, 1997), 65.

7. Honor Books Editors, *God's Little Devotional Book for Teachers* (Colorado Springs: Honor Books, 1999), 145.

8. Stuart A. Herrington, *Traitors Among Us: Inside the Spy Catcher's World* (New York: Harvest Books, 2000), 388.

9. George Barna, "Americans Donate Billions to Charity, But Giving to Churches Has Declined," The Barna Group, April 25, 2005, http://www.barna.org/barna-update/article/5-barna-update/180-americans-donate-billions-to-charity-but-giving-to-churches-has-declined.

10. Barna Group, "Donors Proceed with Caution, Tithing Declines," The Barna Group, May 10, 2011, http://www.barna.org/donorscause-articles/486-donors-proceed-with-caution-tithing-declines.

11. Jeremiah Burroughs, "Secret Sins," in Robert Aitkin Bertram, *A Homiletic Encyclopaedia of Illustrations in Theology and Morals*, 7th ed. (New York: Funk and Wagnalls, 1885), 762.

12. Telephone interview with Pat Williams, July 2012.

13. Phil Taylor, "Life-Changing Victory for Douglas," *Sports Illustrated*, August 2, 2012, http://sportsillustrated.cnn.com/2012/olympics/2012/writers/phil_taylor/08/02/gabby-douglas-olympic-gymnastics/index.html?eref=sihp&sct=hp_t12_a0.

14. Terrell Brown, "Olympics Golden Girl Gabby Douglas Called Marketer's Dream," *CBS News*, August 3, 2012, http://www.cbsnews.com/8301-505263_162-57486059/olympics-golden-girl-gabby-douglas-called-marketers-dream/.

15. Larry Brown, "Gabby Douglas Almost Quit Gymnastics Months Before Olympics," LarryBrownSports.com, August 3, 2012, http://larrybrownsports.com/olympics/gabby-douglas-quit-gymnastics/149018.

16. Daily Mail Reporter, "Gabby Douglas' Secret Heartbreak," *Daily Mail*, August 3, 2012, http://www.dailymail.co.uk/news/article-2183256/Gabby-Douglas-secret-heartbreak-Gold-medal-sensation-tormented-absent-soldier-father--family-split-Olympic-dream.html?ito=feeds-newsxml.

17. Michael W. Chapman, "U.S. Gold Medalist Gabby Douglas: 'I Give All the Glory to God,'" CNSNews.com, August 3, 2012, http://cnsnews.com/news/article/us-gold-medalist-gabby-douglas-i-give-all-glory-god.

18. Ibid.

19. Rabbi Jacob E. Fine, "Refugee Awareness: Lessons from the Biblical Cities of Refuge," MyJewishLearning.com, American Jewish World Service, http://www.myjewishlearning.com/texts/Bible/Weekly_Torah_Portion/masei_ajws.shtml.

20. John R. Wayland, *A Daily Passage Through Mark* (Houston, TX: Whitecaps Media, 2004), 126.

21. A.B. Earle, *Selected Sermon Illustrations from the Writings of Absalom Backas (A.B.) Earle and the Writings of J. Wilbur Chapman*, http://wesley.nnu.edu/wesleyctr/books/0101-0200/HDM0104.PDF.

About Michael Youssef

Michael Youssef was born in Egypt and came to America in his late twenties in 1977. He received a master's degree in theology from Fuller Theological Seminary in California and a PhD in social anthropology from Emory University. Michael served for nearly ten years with the Haggai Institute, traveling around the world teaching courses in evangelism and church leadership to church leaders. He rose to the position of managing director at the age of thirty-one. The family settled in Atlanta, and in 1984, Michael became a United States citizen, fulfilling a dream he had held for many years.

Dr. Youssef founded The Church of The Apostles in 1987 with fewer than forty adults with the mission to "equip the saints and seek the lost." The church has since grown to a congregation of over three thousand. This church on a hill was the launching pad for Leading The Way, an international ministry whose radio and television programs are heard by millions at home and abroad.

For more on Michael Youssef, The Church of The Apostles, and Leading The Way, visit apostles.org and www.leadingtheway.org.

Leading the Way Through the Bible Commentary Series

About the Series: The Leading the Way Through the Bible commentary series will not only increase readers' Bible knowledge, but it will motivate readers to apply God's Word to the problems of our hurting world and to a deeper and more obedient walk with Jesus Christ. The writing is lively, informal, and packed with stories that illustrate the truth of God's Word. The Leading the Way series is a call to action—and a call to the exciting adventure of living for Christ.

LEADING THE WAY THROUGH DANIEL

Daniel lived as an exile in a hostile country, yet when he committed himself in faith to serve his limitless God, he achieved the impossible. How did Daniel maintain his bold witness for God in spite of bullying and intimidation? How did he prepare himself for the tests and temptations of life?

Like Daniel, believers today live in a culture that is hostile to biblical values. It takes great courage and faith to live as followers of Christ in a post-Christian world characterized by moral depravity, injustice, idolatry, and more. In *Leading the Way Through Daniel*, Michael Youssef passionately shows readers that the resources Daniel relied on are equally available to them.

Sound teaching, vibrant illustrations, and a brisk conversational style will enable readers to take the truths of the book of Daniel and apply them to the pressures, trials, and temptations they face in today's culture.

LEADING THE WAY THROUGH EPHESIANS

Throughout the book of Ephesians, Paul refers to "the riches of God's grace," "our riches in Christ," and "the riches of his glory" as he reminds believers of the spiritual treasures they already possess in Christ.

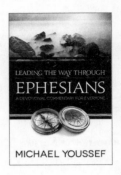

Leading the Way Through Ephesians applies these great truths in such practical areas of the Christian life as

- enduring trials, suffering, and persecution
- maintaining the unity of the church through Christian love
- living out the gospel in our marriages and family relationships
- praying with power
- maintaining our armor against the attacks of Satan

Through sound teaching, vibrant illustrations, a brisk conversational style, and a discussion guide that applies God's truth to the realities of the twenty-first century, *Leading the Way Through Ephesians* will show readers the way to a stronger, more active, more dynamic faith.

Leading the Way Through Galatians

It's tempting for Christians to think they can experience God's life and power through church attendance, religious symbols and rituals, and good deeds. But as the book of Galatians makes clear, religion means nothing unless believers are connected to the *source* of God's life and power.

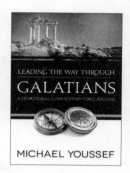

In *Leading the Way Through Galatians*, Michael Youssef applies Paul's message to the churches in Galatia to the challenge of living as authentic Christians in the twenty-first century. The message of the gospel is a message of freedom from the law, freedom from bondage to sin, freedom from fear, freedom from judgment, and freedom from the need to perform and please others.

Through stories and contemporary insights, the timeless truths of Galatians will take on a new and powerful meaning as today's readers learn to apply this liberating message to everyday life and everyday situations.

To learn more about Harvest House books and
to read sample chapters, log on to our website:

www.harvesthousepublishers.com

HARVEST HOUSE PUBLISHERS
EUGENE, OREGON